bread   222

onion soup   80

Scallions green
chile rolls   226
12 muffins

onion - apple   120

Chicken livers + onions   97

onion biscuits   142

Rye bread — 144

Lilies
of the
Kitchen

Lilies
of the
Kitchen

BARBARA BATCHELLER

Recipes Celebrating Onions, Garlic,
Leeks, Shallots, Scallions,
and Chives

WITH A FOREWORD BY WOLFGANG PUCK

ILLUSTRATIONS BY LAUREN JARRETT

ST. MARTIN'S PRESS
NEW YORK

Editor: Toni Lopopolo
Assistant Editor: Jack Cararela
Production Editor: Amelie Littell
Copy Editor: Joan Whitman
Design by Mina Greenstein

Library of Congress Cataloging in Publication Data
Batcheller, Barbara.
    Lilies of the kitchen.
    1. Cookery (Onions) 2. Cookery (Garlic) 3. Cookery
(Leeks) 4. Cookery (Herbs) I. Title.
TX803.05B37 1986   641.6'526   85–25182
ISBN 0–312–48618–9

First Edition

10 9 8 7 6 5 4 3 2 1

CONTENTS

1 A Celebration of Garlic

2 The Incomparable Onion

3 *The Gilded Lilies*

4 Desserts: Wicked and Virtuous

Appendix

ACKNOWLEDGMENTS

To Joanna Barnes, my affectionate thanks for setting my feet on this path, her constant encouragement, and writing the Preface.

A big bouquet for my friend Janis Penslar for her endless good humor, aid and counsel, and skillful editing. She made writing this book about the lilies into a piece of cake. Blessings! . . . and a very special thank you to Wolf, for being there and writing the Foreword.

PREFACE

by Joanna Barnes

It was through Ursula Andress that I first met Barbara Batcheller. Ursula and I were both young actresses, new to Hollywood then. I had graduated from Smith College only weeks earlier, prepared for a career as a writer, never having acted at all, when by a series of nearly preposterous events I found myself making a living in the world of movie magic. I felt like Alice fallen down the rabbit hole. Still more magic was in store for me when Ursula, my new (and today still valued) friend, took me one day to Barbara's house with the promise that I would find it and its owner nothing short of extraordinary.

At the dead end of a commonplace Los Angeles street lined with average stucco bungalows and some palm trees, nearly hidden by planting, stood a high wall with a wooden gate strung with small brass bells. Unlatched, it tinkled open to reveal a place so special that I was reminded at once of the classic children's book, *The Secret Garden,* and of how in that story an obscure garden gate opened the way to adventure, friendship, and enduring affection.

And that is exactly what happened.

Inside the gate was a two-story house of silvery, weathered barn siding lushly overgrown with greenery. The vagaries of many previous owners (including Preston Sturges, the noted director) and of occasional earth tremors had given the place a unique character. The upstairs rooms had a noticeable list to them, and the surface of the brick patio was decidedly erratic. To add to its free-form appearance, flowers ran rampant in masses of colliding colors. Bougainvillea, delphinium, poppies, begonias, geraniums (rose geraniums for flavoring), and jasmine grew like weeds inside these garden walls. Trumpet vine spiraled around sun-splashed columns, and clusters of pungent eucalyptus trees towered over shady porches.

Inside, the house was no less striking. Barbara's domestic talents were irrepressible. Beautiful crewelwork tapestries, needlepoint pillows, and whimsical banners made it quite the liveliest establishment I had ever seen. Lively it was, too, for it was perpetually changing. A pale blue wash over the rough-paneled living room walls, a huge basket filled with bolts of motley fabrics plunked next to the fireplace in the dining room, just for the heck—and the color —of it.

In my memory, however, it is the kitchen (and what came forth from it) that is the most vivid. It had a higgledy-piggledy brick floor, brightly painted cabinets and tiled counters on which savory meats marinated in glazed pottery casseroles, puff paste dough was readied on cool slabs of well-worn marble and cornucopias of fresh vegetables waited to be pared, parboiled, or puréed. The stately six-burner stove had no less than four ovens with a warming oven to boot. Above the diamond-paned windows hung dozens of baskets of dried herbs. Fresh ones grew on the sills. And presiding over this glorious festival of food was Barbara herself.

I trust she will not be offended if I say that even then, in her thirties, she reminded me of the madcap Madame Arcarti in the Noel Coward comedy *Blithe Spirit.* She approached her work with the slightly zany, spontaneous delight of someone born to glory in the art of cooking. And her friends, countless, would amble uninvited through her magical garden gate to congregate in Barbara's kitchen for a cup of coffee or chamomile tea or a taste of a sauce-in-progress, and likely as not be lucky enough to be asked to stay for dinner.

You could learn a lot about good food from Barbara and a lot of other things, too, about joie de vivre and style and the glories of healthy laughter. She was, and is, as dandy a raconteur as a chef.

For the past few years, I've been urging Barbara to set her recipes

—and herself—down on paper. This takes courage, but fortunately she has never been lacking in that admirable quality. Now, at last, stepping out from behind her garden wall and out of the kitchen of the famed Ma Maison restaurant where she won acclaim for her cooking classes, Barbara has come through. It is typical of her to have chosen an unusual subject for this, her first cookbook. Nothing about Barbara has ever been ordinary.

I envy the reader as he or she enters this book much as I entered her secret garden years ago. That charmed hospitality is still present in *Lilies of the Kitchen,* a bouquet of Barbara's unique warmth, savvy and culinary genius. Each page evokes for me, as it will for you, the tempting sights, scents, tastes, and textures of the delights that still draw friends and newcomers alike to her home, where Barbara continues to flourish as the most colorful of all the lilies of the kitchen.

FOREWORD

by Wolfgang Puck

I have always suspected that Barbara was involved in some sort of romance; little did I suspect that the passion that consumed her was for onions. With her style and sense of adventure she has given us a wonderful book about all onions—and believe me, she knows her onions.

There are several very good reasons for this wonderful book on obliging onions and all their delicious relations: vigorous garlic, slender scallions, luxurious leeks, and delicate chives. These edible lilies are a highly versatile family. Onions have a brilliant repertoire of their own, and in addition add subtlety, snap, and dazzle to many, many other foods.

With panache, Barbara elevates the deploringly underrated onion family to its proper royal status. Using a fine eye for physical beauty, a sure sense of simply what tastes good, and a prose that lingers tantalizingly in the mind, Barbara has taken the essential basics of the kitchen and with loving hands has created an indispensable tool for anyone interested in fine cuisine.

It's a rich, satisfying book, full of good recipes, good cooking and life. *Lilies of the Kitchen* is a delight for the reader and an inspiration to any cook. I enjoyed reading it and I think you will too.

INTRODUCTION

I wrote this book just for the fun of it—and it certainly was fun.

The fragrant family has played second banana for entirely too long; it's time the lilies of the kitchen received the starring roles and the applause they so richly and deliciously deserve.

Ah, the marvelous members of the lily family—they offer us an aromatic extravaganza. They are, each one, distinctive. Highly compatible, they mingle easily with each other and are mostly interchangeable. Better a fresh young scallion in hand than languishing after a not-to-be-found perfect shallot—that's what I say. They encourage endless experimentation, from the down-home stew to the most refined, delicate creations we can devise, and they serve us well.

This book is a collection of recipes, some old, some new, and all delicious. They have been tasted, tested, and relished by a procession of husbands, lovers, children, cherished friends, assorted whistlers, and jugglers, and quite a few who came along just for the ride.

So, front and center, obliging satin onions, sleek leeks, mischievous, two-faced garlic, subtle shallots, and slender scallions and chives. The curtain is going up and you're on.

Let's hear it for the lilies of the kitchen!

1 A Celebration of Garlic

Garlic! You stir up, you impel, you cheer; you
are the only condiment, you are the glorious
one, the sovereign extract of the earth.
   —Gustave Coquiot

*A*n impassioned and interminable controversy has raged
around the heads of garlic since that moment lost in the mists of
time when an infamous angel fell from heaven, stamped his left foot
upon the earth, and garlic sprang forth.

It has been revered on one hand and scorned with equal vigor
on the other. To this day the powers of garlic to heal, empower,
and protect are as highly touted as they were in that long-lost time.

During its long, eccentric history, garlic has been enthusiastically
prescribed for a volume of ailments, physical and spiritual, and
equally favored as a powerful talisman against all manner of evil.
For instance:

Aristophanes heartily recommended garlic as a restorative for
failing masculine powers, and as an aid in the sport of Venus. How's
that for starters?

The Roman historian Pliny lists no less than sixty-one medicinal
uses for garlic.

Vampires flee from it.

Garlic will cure a cold.

Garlic, it is also said, will cure warts, fainting spells, the bites of
snakes and insects, improve the circulation, alleviate high blood
pressure, ward off the evil eye, keep the fleas off Fido, render the
garden free of pests, and grow hair.

Today the myths, legends, and counsel abound and proliferate, and great quantities of garlic are surely being channeled to the medical scientists who are busily testing the historic claims of the folk healers. Meanwhile the faithful who continue to take garlic in many forms are grateful for the comfort it gives them.

For our present purpose it's only important to remember that garlic is not only good for you, but brings a deep, mellow flavor and an alluring aroma to much that you cook—with the possible exception of ice cream. No doubt some fanatic somewhere is doing just that—adding garlic to ice cream. Be thankful that you escape his improvisations.

This brings us to cooks and cooking.

Garlic has been the soul of peasant cooking for as long as peasants have cooked and garlic has flourished. It is the most widely used herb in the world. With the production of garlic up 1,000 percent in the last two years, it's clear that it is being used for more than peasant casseroles, folk remedies, and magic spells.

The Chinese, no slouch in the kitchen, honor garlic as the yang in the yin-yang of their culinary art.

In Mediterranean countries, garlic is used with characteristically Latin ardor.

Garlic, in fact, has been used lavishly all over this bright green earth ever since its gleeful discovery—everywhere except Japan, where it continues to be used solely as an honorable medicinal herb.

Garlic has infiltrated even the trendiest circles, where innovative chefs of both nouvelle and haute persuasions use it freely and with distinction, creating a whole repertoire of sophisticated garlic dishes—refined, elegant, and delicious.

The renaissance of cooking as an indoor-outdoor sport and social skill has surely opened our noses to garlic's redolent delights. But whether rowdy or refined, used with subtlety or gusto, for itself alone or to jazz up everything from artichokes to zucchini, we might as well think of garlic as a vegetable and get on with this cookbook.

Technique

Garlic is the ketchup of intellectuals.
—Unknown

There is no substitute for fresh garlic. It's always available, so pass up those scraggly little plastic-wrapped packets. And don't even bother to bring home the junk labeled "garlic powder" or "garlic salt." They are abominations.

Buy only the garlic with big, plump, firm cloves and tight silky skins; peeling a lot of those itsy-bitsy cloves is a pain. The garlic with lavender skins is my favorite. Most Italian markets carry them, and they are worth searching for. The great big stuff known as elephant garlic is mostly a curiosity and not very good raw or cooked.

Actually there is one dried form of garlic you may wish to try— dried sliced garlic. If you are lucky enough to live in a city with an Oriental grocery store, you'll find it there. It is fragrant, pungent, and delicious. While you're there, also be on the lookout for sweet pickled garlic and shallots, and for packages of crisp, fried shredded shallots.

Garlic has a high oil content and will keep well for a month or so in an airy place out of the sun. Dampness is the bane of garlic, so keep it away from stove and sink. Never store it in the refrigerator and, please, don't freeze it—freezing renders it mushy and acrid.

Braided strings of garlic are decorative and handy if you use it like I do. But inspect them carefully and be certain that they are firm, sproutless, and have no signs of softness or discoloration.

It is undeniably true that garlic changes its character depending on how it's treated. The amount of garlic you use is second only to the manner in which you choose to prepare it. Half a clove of garlic in a salad dressing has a more penetrating flavor and aroma than half a pound of garlic braised or roasted with a chicken. And consider this—one clove of garlic is ten times stronger pushed through a garlic press than one clove minced fine with a good sharp knife. Ten times! Something about the essential oils and sulfur, though the technicalities needn't concern us here, just the outcome. Speaking of presses, I think they're more trouble than they're worth. They are a drag to clean and the garlic is rendered strong and acrid.

Peeling garlic is a simple task. To peel just a few cloves, place the flat side of a heavy knife over a clove and rap your fist smartly down onto the blade. You can then easily slip off the skin. You'll learn quickly just how much force to use—too much and the garlic is mashed; you just want to break the seal of the skin.

To ensure ending up with a whole perfect clove, simply nip off the ends of the clove and strip away the peel with the knife edge.

To peel several cloves at a time, drop the unpeeled cloves in boiling water for 30 seconds, rinse under cold water, drain, and peel the skins off easily.

One clove of garlic will yield approximately one teaspoon minced.

Here's an easy way to mince garlic: Peel the clove and then lay it on your working surface. Slice it into pieces and then chop until you have achieved the size mince you wish.

Puréed garlic is essential to vinaigrette dressing. To reduce a clove to the consistency of thick cream, mash it with a quarter teaspoon of salt with the tip of a table knife or fork tines until you have a smooth purée.

If you're not a fanatic about garlic yet, consider blanching the little devils before adding them to your dish. This simple procedure will render them socially acceptable with their flavor and aroma intact. Simply plunge the unpeeled cloves into two cups of boiling water for a minute or two; snip off the ends after rinsing them in cold water. They will slip right out of their skins, ready to go, suave and flavorful.

For an even more subtle finish, double- (or triple) blanch them. After following the above procedure, bring a second (or third) pot of water to the boil, drop in the cloves for a minute, then drain. Perfectly gentled.

To reconstitute the Oriental dried sliced garlic, place the amount you need in a small bowl and cover with very hot water. When soft, drain *well.* Use like fresh garlic or sauté in a little oil or butter until light golden blond.

Be careful not to allow your garlic to get too brown or it will be bitter and, God forbid, don't burn it. If you do, throw it out and start over.

If you seek only a hint, a faint whisper, a memory, use whole, peeled cloves and remove them from your dish when they have lent their essence to it, after a minute or two. Or try rubbing a heated serving platter for fish, chicken, or steamed vegetables with a clove of garlic for a delicate flavor.

For a lustier flavor, try adding minced garlic to your dish a few minutes before it's finished—*et voilà!* Garlic heaven, fresh and jazzy.

Speaking of minced garlic, how about *hachis*—the piquant garnish from southwestern France? Just finely chop a couple of cloves of garlic together with a handful of parsley leaves and strew over grilled meats or roast chicken.

By the way, garlic is a fine salt substitute, especially good when cooking for friends with high blood pressure.

Make a potion of minced garlic, parsley, a fine light olive oil, and whatever fresh herbs you like, and strew it over a dish of crisp steamed vegetables. Whoopee!

Keep a jar of garlic oil on hand at all times. In a clean pint jar with a well-fitting lid, place two large heads of garlic, separated, unpeeled, and lightly crushed. Pour over them enough fine light olive oil to fill the jar within one-half inch of the top. Allow to stand, tightly covered, in a nice dim place—out of the sun, for heaven's sake. Use it as you wish for sautéing, to dress a salad, or to lift freshly cooked pasta to new heights. As you use the oil, replenish it, and this fragrant condiment will live on and on.

If your basil is growing furiously, try this: wash the leaves, dry them gently with paper towels, pack them firmly into a half-pint jar to within an inch of the top, and then fill to the top with a fine light olive oil. Cover tightly. In a few days you will have a jar of gorgeous emerald oil; the very essence of fresh basil, to use as you please. Drizzle it on French bread and make a sandwich. Splash it on pasta. Tomatoes sing with it. As you use it, add enough new oil to keep the leaves covered.

The Glory of Garlic

It is not an exaggeration to say that, geograph-
ically, peace and happiness begin where garlic
is used in cooking.

. . . so says Marcel Boulestin, the celebrated French gastronome,
chef, and bon vivant. I won't argue with him and neither will the
citizens of Gilroy, California, the garlic capital of America, where
every year, late in the summer, at the time of their prodigious
harvest, they produce their famous garlic festival.

Garlic lovers from all over are joyously drawn to this aromatic
arena to taste, even wallow in garlicky delights. Last summer they
used six and one-half tons of the fragrant bulb cooking up hundreds
of dishes that they ladled out to the happy garlic fanatics. That's a
lot of garlic, but a tiny part of the annual harvest produced here;
as we speak, it approaches 200 million pounds. And God knows
how much the French produce in their garlic capital, Arleux, where
they annually regale their own 70,000 fanatics.

After the Fact

The offensiveness of the breath of him that hath
eaten garlick will lead you by the nose to the
knowledge thereof.
—Nicholas Culpeper

To remove the garlic scent from your hands, try rubbing them with
a little salt, then wash them with soap and water. Or rub them with
a cut lemon.

The ancient Greeks freshened their breath by chewing parsley
after a feast of garlic—it still works. Fresh mint, a roasted coffee

bean, a slice of orange or lemon peel, or, best of all, a bit of chocolate, are also effective.

> There is no such thing as too much garlic.
> —Barbara Batcheller

Subtlety isn't garlic's long suit. How such a small, delicate-looking package can pack such a wallop is a wonder. Happily it is possible to use huge amounts of garlic and produce a distinctive dish with alluring, mellow flavor and aroma.

So even if garlic isn't one of your passions at the moment, and the amount of garlic called for in some of these recipes alarms you, go ahead and give them a whirl anyhow—you may be in for some delicious surprises.

Just remember that there are no hard and fast rules; it's your personal taste that is important. So experiment. After all, it's your cooking.

FIRST COURSES

GARLIC TAPENADE

Serves four

Serve this lusty sauce with crackers, unsalted bread, or toast triangles as an accompaniment to salad. Try it as a luxurious dip for raw or lightly parboiled vegetables, stuffed into tomatoes or hard-boiled egg halves, or tossed with cold pasta.

2 garlic cloves, blanched and peeled
¼ pound black olives, pitted
2 ounces anchovy fillets, soaked in 3 tablespoons milk
2 ounces tuna fish (Italian preferred), drained
½ tablespoon dry mustard
½ cup olive oil
1 ½ tablespoons brandy
Freshly ground black pepper
Pinch of mace or nutmeg
2 tablespoons small capers

Put the garlic, olives, drained anchovy fillets, tuna, and mustard powder in a food processor or blender and process to a smooth paste.

Add oil in a thin stream while continuing to process. Add brandy, pepper, and spice and blend again. Remove from processor. Add capers and mix well to combine. Tapenade will keep, refrigerated, for about one week.

To serve, place tapenade in an attractive small serving bowl or earthenware pot and surround with crackers, toast, or bread.

OEUFS À L'AILLADE

Serves six

This charming title just means deviled eggs—but what deviled eggs! They are a reliable first course, the main event of a simple lunch served with salad and cold meat, or a savory addition to a picnic.

6 eggs
10 garlic cloves, peeled
3 anchovy fillets, drained
3 tablespoons olive oil
Dash of red wine vinegar
Salt

Freshly ground black pepper
1 tablespoon minced fresh parsley
1 tablespoon tiny capers
Sprigs of watercress
Baby radishes with leaves still
    attached

Place the eggs and garlic in a pan of cold water to cover. Bring to a boil and cook over medium heat 10 minutes. Peel the eggs and cut in half lengthwise. Remove yolks and reserve. Cut a thin slice from the bottom of each white so it doesn't wobble on the serving plate. Set aside.

Cool garlic cloves and place in a mortar with anchovy fillets and egg yolks. Pound to a paste with the pestle. (You may also blend them in a food processor, but the consistency of the mortar and pestle method is superior.)

Slowly beat in the olive oil. Add vinegar, salt and pepper to taste, and parsley. Blend in capers but do not mash.

Spoon the mixture into the egg whites. Serve garnished with sprigs of watercress and baby radishes, each with a small leaf attached.

MUSHROOMS PROVENÇALE

Serves six

A light, fresh first course. Serve them on a leaf of red cabbage or radicchio. Or try them as part of an antipasto.

2 pounds mushrooms	*Freshly ground black pepper*
½ cup olive oil, or half olive and half peanut	*Sprig or two of fresh rosemary, marjoram, or thyme*
½ cup chopped parsley	*2 garlic cloves, peeled and finely minced*
½ cup day-old bread crumbs	*Lemon juice*
Salt	

Wipe the mushrooms clean with damp paper towels. Pare off scarred stem ends. Twist out stems and chop. Slice or quarter caps depending on size.

Heat olive oil in a heavy skillet and add mushrooms. Sauté over medium heat, stirring occasionally, until lightly browned. Add parsley, bread crumbs, salt, pepper, and herbs. Toss gently until heated through.

Serve mushrooms sprinkled with fresh minced garlic and lemon juice to taste.

MUSHROOMS MARINATED WITH GARLIC, LEMON, AND BAY

Serves six

Keep a jar of these tender, fragrant morsels in the refrigerator. Hand them out with drinks or as an emergency first course.

⅔ cup olive oil

½ cup water

Juice of 2 lemons

3 bay leaves

3 garlic cloves, peeled

6 black peppercorns

1 teaspoon salt

Sprig of fresh parsley

1 pound small fresh mushrooms

Bring all the ingredients but mushrooms to a boil in a heavy sauce-pan. Reduce heat and simmer 10 minutes. Pour through a fine strainer and return liquid to pan.

Wipe mushrooms with damp paper towels. Pare toughened ends from stems. Twist stems carefully from caps. Simmer caps and stems in marinade for 10 minutes. Cool.

Transfer mushrooms and marinade to a covered refrigerator container and chill for one to two days. Serve chilled or, preferably, at room temperature on individual serving plates with thin toast triangles spread with Garlic Tapenade (see page 9) and garnished with a leaf or two of watercress.

OCTOBER SAUCE FOR PASTA

*Serves six as a first course,
four as an entrée*

One warm day in Rome, a dashing Italian actor who always wore Western gear, complete with jingling spurs, made this zingy pasta for me with his customary élan. For a long time afterward I thought that it was his charm that made it taste so fine. Much later, however, I made it on my own without the music of his jingling spurs and, what do you know, it was still a fine dish!

3 garlic cloves, chopped

1 tin anchovies, oil and all

1 cup white wine

Juice of ½ lemon

½ cup best olive oil

1 pound linguine, fresh or dried

⅓ cup minced fresh parsley

Salt

Freshly ground black pepper

8–10 large basil leaves

Place the garlic, anchovies, and wine in a saucepan and reduce to about 1/2 cup over moderate to high heat.

Add the lemon juice and oil, stir, and set aside.

Prepare pasta and drain.

Just before serving, pour the sauce over the hot pasta, add parsley, and toss to coat. Taste for seasonings. Garnish with basil leaves before serving.

AFTERTHOUGHT: You might like to add some chopped fresh tomatoes to the pasta before you serve it.

PASTA WITH OIL AND GARLIC

Serves six as a first course

Heaven for garlic purists! This is the time, if there ever was one, to use a fine fresh pasta and the very best olive oil.

1 pound thin pasta (spaghetti, linguine, etc.)	*Salt*
	Freshly ground black pepper
10–12 garlic cloves, minced	*Handful of minced fresh parsley*
¼ cup best olive oil	*Imported Parmesan or Romano*
3 tablespoons butter, softened	*cheese, freshly grated*

Plunge pasta into at least 4 quarts boiling water and cook to your taste.

Meanwhile, sauté the garlic in olive oil over low heat for 2 to 3 minutes, until garlic just begins to show a golden color. Remove from heat and set aside.

Drain pasta well and return to pot off the heat. Add butter and toss with hot pasta. Season to taste with salt and a grinding or two of black pepper. Add garlic and oil and parsley; toss again. Taste once more for seasonings and adjust as necessary. (There is nothing duller than underseasoned pasta.)

Serve immediately in individual heated shallow soup bowls, accompanied by grated Parmesan and a pepper mill.

AFTERTHOUGHT: Please, never blaspheme pasta by rinsing it.

ANGEL HAIR PASTA WITH GARLIC-WALNUT SAUCE

Serves eight as a first course

Twittering behind our fans, shall we mention nutrition and complex carbohydrates? I think not.

⅓ cup olive or walnut oil
½ cup chopped walnuts
6 garlic cloves, peeled
Salt
Freshly ground black pepper

1 tablespoon tiny capers
1 pound angel hair pasta (this
   is the thinnest pasta)
Few leaves of watercress

Heat the olive oil in a small skillet and add the chopped walnuts. Sauté gently until the nuts begin to take on a little color. Add the garlic cloves and continue to sauté until the garlic is golden and soft and the nuts are light brown. Add salt and pepper to taste. Remove from heat and stir in capers.

Cook the pasta in rapidly boiling water until it is barely tender, about a minute or so. Drain.

Toss the pasta with the garlic-walnut mixture. Taste for seasoning and adjust if necessary. Serve at once, garnished with a few watercress leaves.

AFTERTHOUGHT: Try this pasta as a first course, followed by paillard of chicken with lemon and tarragon and a salad of cold vegetables. Perhaps a mango mousse for dessert?

ROASTED GARLIC WITH CHÈVRE

Serves six

Slowly roasting garlic with lots of olive oil and salt brings out a surprising sweetness and a mellow, nutty flavor. The fun follows when you and your guests pull off the cloves and pinch them out of their papery skins and onto rounds of crusty bread spread with herbed chèvre, or one that you have marinated in olive oil to cover with a pinch or two of dried herbes de Provence.

6 *heads garlic*	6 *ounces chèvre (goat cheese)*
Olive oil	*Cream*
Butter	*Chives and fresh parsley*
Salt	*Dried mixed herbs*
Freshly ground black pepper	

Preheat oven to 300°F.

Score around the middle of six heads of garlic, being careful not to cut into the cloves. Remove the top half of the outer layer of skin from each head, exposing the cloves, and leave the bottom half intact. Place the heads, exposed side up, in a small baking pan.

Pour a generous tablespoon of olive oil over each head, dot with butter, and season with salt and pepper to taste. Cover the pan with aluminum foil and place it in the preheated oven. Bake for 30 minutes, remove the cover, and continue baking for an additional hour, basting frequently, until the heads are very tender. If the heads are very large, the baking could require an additional 15 or 20 minutes.

When done, remove them from the oven and allow to cool to room temperature.

While the heads are cooling, prepare the chèvre. Put the cheese in a small bowl and blend in enough cream to achieve a spreadable consistency. Add freshly minced chives and parsley to taste, and a pinch or two of your favorite dried herbs. If you are using marinated goat cheese, nothing more is needed as the oil improves its spreadability, and the herbs have already done their work.

Serve the whole heads of garlic with their oil, accompanied by a crusty loaf and the cheese. Dip the bread in the oil, spread on the cheese, and squeeze on the garlic pearls.

AFTERTHOUGHT Make an extra head when roasting garlic. When cool, just pinch out the cloves and keep in a tightly covered glass container in the refrigerator. You'll have garlic ready whenever you need it, and it keeps for a long while.

SNAILS WITH GARLIC BUTTER

Serves four

The classic.

12 tablespoons butter, at room
  temperature
4 garlic cloves, minced
4 shallots, minced
2 tablespoons finely chopped
  parsley

Salt
Freshly ground black pepper
4 dozen canned snails (and their
  shells)

Preheat oven to 425°F.

Cream the butter and blend in the garlic, shallots, and parsley. Season to taste with salt and pepper.

Place one snail into each shell. Fill each shell opening with the butter mixture.

Arrange snails on ovenproof snail plates. Bake for 6 or 7 minutes. Serve immediately with thinly sliced toasted French bread.

ESCARGOTS À LA MISTRAL
(Snails with Tomatoes Concasse)

Serves six as a first course

A toast to the person who thought up this way with snails! Always a great favorite with the gents in my cooking classes—the rascals nearly ate them up before I could arrange them on the croutons. They *said* they were testing the seasoning, but the servings were noticeably smaller if I didn't keep a sharp watch on them as they repeatedly "tested the seasoning."

A word of caution—this is serious. Allow the snails to get hot in the sauce, but don't boil them, for heaven's sake, or you might as well use Pink Pearl erasers.

36 *canned snails, drained*
12 *tablespoons unsalted butter*
2 *garlic cloves, minced*
¾ *cup Tomatoes Concasse (recipe*
  follows)

½ *teaspoon green peppercorns,*
  chopped
Salt
Pernod to taste
Minced fresh parsley

Rinse the snails under cold running water. Drain thoroughly.

Melt butter in a heavy skillet and add the minced garlic. Sauté for about 1 minute over moderate heat, but do not brown. Add tomatoes *concasse* and heat for 3 or 4 minutes.

Add snails to pan and heat slowly for 5 minutes. Remove from heat. Stir in peppercorns, salt to taste, and a splash of Pernod. Transfer the mixture to an attractive serving dish and sprinkle with minced parsley. Serve with toasted French bread, Croûtes, (page 68), or Garlic Pita Toasts (page 64).

TOMATOES CONCASSE

Aside from being a splendid addition to cooked dishes and sauces, *concasse* is delicious as an accompaniment to cold foods, or used as a garnish. Simply peel, seed, juice, and finely chop as many perfectly ripe tomatoes as you need. Salt to taste. Vary the *concasse* with minced shallots or scallions, with fresh herbs, or dress with fragrant olive oil and a bit of wine vinegar.

SOUPS

SPANISH GARLIC SOUP

Serves four

This may well be Spain's answer to the French hangover remedy. In any case, it has its own character and garlic essence.

4 large garlic cloves, peeled
2 cans beef broth
2 cups water
1 cup dry sherry
Salt

Freshly ground black pepper
4 slices French bread
4 tablespoons butter, softened
2 tablespoons freshly grated
   Parmesan cheese

Put garlic and beef broth in a large saucepan. Bring to a boil, cover, and simmer until garlic is soft, approximately 15 minutes. Remove garlic and set aside.

Add water and sherry to broth. Taste for seasonings and correct. Heat to serving temperature and keep warm.

Meanwhile, toast bread on one side under the broiler. Remove and butter untoasted side. Mash softened garlic and spread over bread. Sprinkle with cheese. Broil until brown and bubbly, 30 seconds to 1 minute.

Place one slice of toasted bread in each individual serving bowl. Ladle hot soup over bread and serve.

GARLIC SOUP OF ARLEUX

Serves four generously

During the garlic festival in Arleux, this soup is ladled out freely and for a price. You can produce your own garlic festival, and why not start off with this wonderful garlicky treat?

10–12 large garlic cloves, thinly
   sliced
1½ cups minced onions
3 tablespoons unsalted butter
1 tablespoon flour
5 cups chicken broth, warmed
2 eggs, separated

4 teaspoons red wine vinegar
Salt
Freshly ground black pepper
Minced fresh parsley
8 slices lightly toasted French
   bread, drizzled with olive oil,
   peppered to taste

Sauté the garlic and onions in butter over medium heat until golden, about 5 minutes. Lower heat and add the flour, stirring constantly. Cook until lightly colored. Remove from heat.

Add broth gradually, reserving 1/2 cup. Stir briskly until well blended to avoid lumps. Return to heat and bring to a boil. Simmer, uncovered, 30 minutes.

Lightly beat egg whites until frothy. Add remaining 1/2 cup of broth and blend. Set aside.

Beat yolks separately with vinegar. Set aside.

Reheat soup to boiling. Ladle 1 cup of the hot soup into the yolk and vinegar mixture and combine. Reserve.

Remove soup from heat. Pour in egg-white mixture in a thin, steady stream while whisking gently to form threadlike strands. Return soup to barest simmer, and stir in yolk mixture. Blend, stirring gently, while soup barely simmers. Be very careful not to allow soup to boil or eggs will curdle.

When soup is creamy, remove from heat, adjust seasoning, and serve immediately, garnished with minced parsley (or wear a wreath of it as the Romans did). Pass toasted bread slices.

AFTERTHOUGHT: Chinese dried sliced garlic works just fine in this soup. Reconstitute it in very hot water.

SOUPE À L'AIL

Serves six

The legendary French remedy for the hangover and *la grippe.* Neither is required, however, to relish a bowl of this admirable soup. *À vôtre santé!*

24 garlic cloves, peeled	*Salt*
2 tablespoons olive oil	*Freshly ground black pepper*
2 quarts chicken broth	*4 egg yolks, beaten*
Pinch each of nutmeg, cloves,	
and grated lemon peel	

In a heavy soup kettle, lightly sauté garlic cloves in oil until a pale golden blond.

Add chicken broth and spices and bring to a boil. Lower heat and simmer slowly for about 20 minutes. Cool slightly.

Purée in a blender or food processor and return to the kettle. Heat slightly and add beaten egg yolks gradually, stirring constantly. Do not allow soup to boil.

Serve immediately. You may enjoy this lovely soup poured over toasted French bread.

COLD GARLIC-WALNUT SOUP

Serves four generously

This soup is heavenly cold or hot.

1 cup toasted walnuts	*Salt*
3 fat garlic cloves, blanched and	*Freshly ground black pepper*
peeled	*½ cup heavy cream*
1 quart boiling chicken broth	*1 tablespoon minced parsley*

Place the toasted walnuts and the garlic in a blender and whirl until smooth. Add half the chicken broth and blend.

Pour the soup into a tureen and add the rest of the hot broth. Check the seasoning; add more if necessary. Allow to cool before adding the cream. Chill thoroughly before serving; garnish with a sprinkling of minced parsley.

AFTERTHOUGHT: Serve this as a first course followed by braised lamb shanks with dried apricots, and a salad of watercress and crisp bean sprouts with Mustard Vinaigrette (page 52).

EVENING SOUP WITH GRUYÈRE

Serves four

This soup makes a light supper accompanied by slices of pâte, crusty bread, a bright green salad, and a dessert of oranges with rosemary (page 235).

5 cups beef broth (homemade or canned)
1 cup dry red wine
6 garlic cloves, finely minced
2 bay leaves
1¼ cups dry bread crumbs, homemade or packaged (unseasoned)

Salt
Freshly ground black pepper
4 tablespoons butter
Pinch of nutmeg
½ cup heavy cream
1 cup grated Gruyère cheese

Bring broth and wine to a boil in a soup kettle. Add garlic, bay leaves, and bread crumbs. Lower heat and simmer, covered, 30 minutes.

Remove soup from heat and discard bay leaves. Add salt and pepper to your taste and add butter and nutmeg. Stir in the cream and gently reheat the soup. Do *not* let it boil.

When heated through, serve immediately. Pass the grated Gruyère separately, encouraging your guests to use it lavishly.

PENICILLIN PROVENÇALE

Serves one

This is simple to prepare, light and refreshing, and, as an added boon, is an old-time remedy for both colds and the misery of a hangover.

1 small onion, chopped
4–6 garlic cloves, peeled
½ teaspoon grated fresh ginger
1 cup water

Salt
Freshly ground black pepper
Large pinch of finely minced mixed fresh herbs

Bring all the ingredients except herbs to a boil in a small saucepan. Lower heat, cover, and simmer together until onions and garlic are tender, about 20 minutes.

Strain. Serve broth hot garnished with fresh herbs (use parsley, rosemary, chives, oregano; whatever you fancy). For intense suffering, serve this soup with a tot of brandy and a box of Kleenex. *À votre santé!*

PAPPA RUSTICA

Serves eight

The Italians know how to live—and this recipe is living proof.

6 garlic cloves, chopped
¼ teaspoon dried red pepper
　flakes (or more)
⅓ cup olive oil
2 pounds ripe tomatoes, peeled,
　seeded, and chopped
1 loaf stale, dry bread (French
　or Italian)

5 cups chicken broth
Large handful of mixed fresh
　herbs (see Afterthought)
Salt
Freshly ground black pepper
Cruet of fine, fruity olive oil

In a large heavy pot, sauté the garlic and red pepper flakes in the olive oil. Add the tomatoes and simmer 15 minutes.

Cut the bread into large cubes (1 1/2 inches or so) and add to the pot. Add the chicken broth, mixed herbs, salt, and pepper to taste. Stir well until all the liquid is absorbed by the bread. Cover and simmer over low heat for 10 minutes. Turn off heat and let rest for an hour.

Reheat before serving with plenty of olive oil for your guests to pour over this soulful dish.

AFTERTHOUGHT:　Use whatever fresh herbs are available, but use only fresh. Try a mix of rosemary, basil, oregano, chives, and a few mint leaves.

BOURRIDE
(Garlic Fish Soup)

Serves eight

A classic Provençal dish. Use whatever kinds of firm, white-fleshed fish look good in the market—haddock, cod, bass, flounder, perch, or halibut.

4½ pounds fish, two or three
  types
3 large leeks, white part only,
  chopped
1 large onion, chopped
1 large carrot, chopped
3 tablespoons olive oil
1½ cups dry white wine
1½ cups water
Juice of ½ lemon
1 teaspoon fennel seed

3 parsley sprigs
1 teaspoon dried thyme
1 teaspoon grated fresh orange
  peel
2 bay leaves
Few grindings of black pepper
Salt
Toasted French bread slices
2 cups Aïoli (page 58)
Fresh parsley, minced

Fillet the fish yourself or have the fishmonger do it for you, saving heads and bones.

Sauté the leeks, onion, and carrot in olive oil in a large heavy soup pot until tender and lightly colored. Add fish heads and bones, the wine, water, lemon juice, fennel, parsley, thyme, orange rind, and bay leaves and bring to a boil, skimming off froth. (There should be enough liquid to cover ingredients. Add more water and/or wine if necessary.) Simmer, uncovered, for 30 minutes.

Strain the stock into a pot, pressing down with the back of a large spoon to extract as much liquid as possible. Discard solids. Bring the stock back to a boil, then a simmer.

While the stock is reheating, cut the fillets into 2-inch-square pieces. Slip the pieces into the simmering broth and let them cook gently about 6 minutes, until just done. Remove them carefully and keep warm, covered, in a low (200°) oven while you finish the soup.

Keep the stock warm, just below a simmer. Spoon about 1 cup of aïoli into a bowl. Add 1 cup of the warm stock and blend well. Pour the aïoli mixture back into the soup, stirring constantly. Do not, repeat *do not,* allow the soup to get anywhere near the boil or you will have scrambled eggs. Taste for salt and adjust as needed.

To serve, place a slice of toasted French bread that has been drizzled with a bit of olive oil in the bottom of a soup plate. Distribute a serving of fish over the toasted round and ladle the soup over all. Sprinkle with parsley. That's one. Do this seven more times and then pass the remaining aïoli. Enjoy!

MEAL FOR MILLIONS
(Or How to Feed a Posse)

Now I'm going to tell you how to make a dish that's a real crowd pleaser—for those times when the posse is breathing hungrily down your neck. Here goes:

Get out your biggest soup pot, fill it with 6 quarts of water and 1 pound of dried Great Northern white beans or cranberry beans (dried limas are okay) that have been soaked overnight, a small ham hock, 3 or 4 unpeeled brown onions, halved and studded here and there with a few cloves, 6 or 8 peeled garlic cloves, and 1 tablespoon salt—a teaspoon of dried red pepper flakes won't hurt either. Toss in your favorite bouquet garni and bring to a boil, then reduce the heat and simmer until the beans are very tender. Lift out half the beans and run them through the blender until they are smooth. Remove the ham and do anything you want with it. You could discard the skin, bones and fat, chop the ham, and return it to the pot. Oh yes, remove the bouquet garni and the onions, including any of the skins that may have slipped off. Adjust the seasoning. Oops, don't forget to return the puréed beans to the pot. Set aside.

Now for the kicker:

Mince 1/3 pound lean salt pork very, very fine. Use your heaviest knife and heat the blade occasionally (with hot water) so that the pork doesn't stick to it. As the meat spreads out, keep turning and folding it toward the center. When you have minced it until it's almost like creamed butter, add 4 to 6 peeled garlic cloves and 2 finely minced onions. Place this mixture in a saucepan and sauté it gently—don't let it brown too much. Add a large can of tomatoes, the Italian ones, or an equal quantity of chopped fresh ones. Let this simmer for half an hour or longer, then set aside and keep warm over a *very* low flame. Remember to toss in 1/2 cup of chopped parsley just before serving.

Begin to reheat the bean soup.

Now, take two bunches of chard or kale, wash carefully, shake off excess moisture, and cut them into big shreds. Sauté in a little olive oil, and when the leaves are shiny with the oil, clap on the pot lid and cook for a couple of minutes, or until they are softened but still a beautiful bright green. Reserve.

Place the soup in a heated tureen. Pass the tomato stuff and the chard separately, and allow each person to dress up his own bowl. Have them top the soup with lashings of freshly grated Parmesan or Romano. Serve with plenty of crusty bread or, better yet, Bruschetta (see page 64), and as much robust red wine as you deem prudent.

A dish worthy of wise men, kings, or your very own posse.

AFTERTHOUGHTS: The basic bean soup is very presentable served with a big bowl of all kinds of vegetables cut into pleasing shapes, and steamed until crisp-tender. Serve them separately, adding as much as you like—try zucchini, string beans, carrots, shredded cabbage, and/or spinach. Crisp and hot french-fried croutons lavishly rubbed with garlic and swished around in the soup are a blessing. Cheese, too. How about grated Gruyère, for instance? Or omit the tomato condiment and try the soup with Aïoli (see page 58) and croutons with lots of parsley and lightly steamed vegetables. Use fresh chopped herbs if your garden is growing furiously. Or how about pesto? And cruets of fine oil and balsamic vinegar. Or? Or?

Forget salad when you serve this soup. Fruit and cheese is the usual thing for dessert—but why not go all out and serve something really wicked (see Desserts).

❦

SOUPE AU POISSON À LA ROUILLE

Serves six

Here is a dish to vanquish the hour of the wolf, or to ornament revels and celebrations. A glorious debauch requiring only the best of everything and, for a while, your undivided attention.

2 pounds mussels or small clams,
  tightly closed, scrubbed and
  debearded
3 pounds fish bones (use any
  saltwater fish except salmon)
1 large carrot, sliced
1 large onion, sliced
1 fennel bulb, chopped
1 shallot, sliced
2 garlic cloves, peeled
1 stalk celery with top, sliced
4 tablespoons olive oil
2 cups dry white wine

1 bouquet garni
1 large can tomatoes, mashed
1 lemon, thinly sliced
Clam juice, as necessary
1 pound sea bass, filleted
1 pound halibut or monkfish,
  filleted
½ pound shrimp, cleaned and
  peeled
6–8 Croûtes (page 68)
1 cup Rouille (page 56)
½ pound imported Gruyère or
  Swiss cheese, grated

Soak the mussels in 4 quarts cold water for 1 hour.

In a large soup pot, over medium heat, sauté fish bones, carrot, onion, fennel, shallot, garlic, and celery in olive oil for 10 minutes.

Deglaze the pan with the wine. Add the bouquet garni, tomatoes, and lemon, and enough water to cover. Bring to a boil, lower heat, and simmer for 45 minutes. Remove from the heat and strain, pressing down on solids to extract their juices. If too much liquid has cooked away, add clam juice.

Return soup to heat and check for seasoning, adjusting if necessary. Bring back to the boil, then lower heat to simmer.

Cut fish into large chunks and add to soup along with the shrimp. Add mussels a minute or so later, and poach all seafood gently until the fish loses its translucence, the shrimp turns pink, and the mussels open, 7 or 8 minutes. Do not overcook or seafood will toughen.

To serve, place a croûte spread generously with rouille in the bottom of each deep soup bowl. Place a portion of the fish and shellfish over the toast. Cover with plenty of grated Gruyère, and ladle very hot soup over all to melt the cheese. Pass additional rouille and cheese at the table, i.e. fire and fall back.

AFTERTHOUGHTS: Any firm-fleshed, nonoily ocean fish will do: ling cod, pollack, flounder, sea perch, snapper, etc. Have your fish man fillet them for you, saving all bones. Ask for extra bones; he'll be happy to give them to you.

By the way, you may also wish to try Knorr's fish bouillon cubes or one of the Japanese instant fish stocks, called *dashi*. Either of these are fine if you don't want to take the time to make your own fish stock.

ENTRÉES

❧

MEXICAN CHICKEN

Serves four to six

If you play your culinary cards right, you'll bring this one in on time and under budget, and thus have plenty of time to retire to your chaise longue to read a spicy novel before dinner. Olé!

1 teaspoon cumin seeds
3 whole chicken breasts, skinned, boned, and halved
Vegetable oil
Salt
Freshly ground black pepper
3 tablespoons olive oil
2 medium onions, sliced thin
3 tablespoons finely chopped, seeded fresh jalapeño peppers

4 garlic cloves, finely minced
2 large ripe tomatoes, seeded and chopped
Flour tortillas, warmed
Guacamole
Sour cream
Salsa fresca (yours or purchased)
Chopped fresh coriander leaves

Preheat oven to 350°F.

Roast the cumin seeds in a dry frying pan over medium heat until they release their fragrance. Remove from heat, crush with a pestle, and set aside.

Brush chicken lightly with oil. Place two breasts on a 12-inch sheet of aluminum foil. Sprinkle with one third of the crushed cumin, and sprinkle with salt and pepper to taste. Seal foil carefully, making sure chicken breasts remain in one layer. Repeat procedure with remaining four breasts. Place foil packets on a cookie sheet.

Bake in oven approximately 25 minutes, or until no longer pink. Remove from oven and allow to cool.

When chicken is cool enough to handle, tear into long, thin strips. Wrap and set aside.

Heat olive oil in a large heavy skillet over medium heat. Add onions and sauté until softened, about 5 minutes. Add peppers and garlic and sauté 2 minutes. Add tomatoes and cook, uncovered, 10 minutes. Add chicken and heat through. Season with salt and freshly ground pepper.

Serve chicken, tortillas, guacamole, sour cream, salsa, and coriander in separate dishes. Have your guests wrap the chicken and condiments in a warm tortilla to eat with their hands. Serve with damp terry-cloth washcloths, rolled and placed in a serving basket. They'll need them.

SMUGGLERS' CHICKEN
(A Gift from Bandits?)

Serves six to eight

This one comes from a long line of smugglers, bandits, and outlaws who, when not about their sly, nefarious activities, apparently retired to their caves and hideouts, did a little cooking, and let the good times roll.

1 large head garlic
2 large lemons
1 teaspoon sugar
1 teaspoon salt
Few sprigs of fresh thyme, oregano and/or marjoram
1 quart water
1½ cups half-and-half
6–8 chicken legs and thighs, attached

Vegetable oil
2 garlic cloves, minced
Salt
Freshly ground black pepper
½ cup Madeira
1 cup chicken broth (homemade or canned)
Minced fresh parsley

Separate garlic head into cloves. Blanch the cloves in boiling water for 2 minutes, drain, and peel. Set aside.

Peel 1 1/2 lemons with a vegetable peeler, reserving unpeeled half for later use. Remove inner white membrane and all seeds. Blanch the peel in boiling water for 1 minute, drain, and set aside.

Slice the lemons. In a large heavy saucepan, combine peeled garlic, lemon peel and slices, sugar, salt, and herbs with the water. Bring to a boil, reduce heat, and simmer, uncovered, 1 to 2 hours, stirring occasionally, until water has almost evaporated and the garlic cloves are golden brown and very tender.

Add half-and-half. Reduce by half, stirring frequently. Strain, pressing down on all solids to extract their juices. Set aside to cool. The sauce can be prepared a day in advance and refrigerated.

Preheat oven to 375°F.

Dry the chicken with paper towels. Pour a few drops of oil into the palms of your hands and lightly oil chicken parts. Place them in a roasting pan and scatter the minced garlic over them. Slice the unpeeled lemon half and strew slices over. Sprinkle with salt and a few grindings of pepper, and roast the chicken in preheated oven for about 30 minutes, or until nicely browned and the juices run clear when the chicken is pricked with a fork (pierce the thickest part of the thigh).

Remove chicken from the oven; turn off heat. Transfer pieces to a serving platter and keep warm, covered with foil.

Deglaze the roasting pan with Madeira over medium-high heat, scraping up all browned bits. Add chicken broth and reduce by half. Strain into a saucepan. Stir in reserved garlic–cream sauce. Reduce slightly over medium-high heat to a creamy sauce. Adjust seasoning by adding a few more drops of lemon juice. Serve at once over warm chicken, garnished with freshly minced parsley.

CHICKEN WITH A SAUCE OF RED ONIONS

Serves four

This is a favorite dish of southwest France. It is simple to prepare and requires only a green salad and your favorite crusty bread to complete the meal. Although it calls for a quartered chicken, it works equally well with a disjointed bird, or veal chops, for that matter.

1 chicken, 3½ to 4 pounds
Salt
Freshly ground black pepper
2–3 tablespoons rendered chicken
    fat (page 173)
3 cups coarsely chopped red
    onions

½ cup diced ham (prosciutto,
    Westphalian, or your own
    leftover baked ham)
1 garlic clove, minced
½ cup dry white wine
Minced chives
Watercress sprigs

Quarter the chicken yourself or have your butcher do it for you. Wipe quarters with damp paper towels. Season with salt and pepper to your taste and set aside.

Heat fat in a large heavy skillet over medium to medium-high heat. Add the chicken and brown on both sides, turning often. When nicely colored, remove chicken to a plate while you prepare the onions.

Lower heat and add onions and ham and cook slowly until onions are tender and transluscent, about 10 minutes. Add garlic and cook a minute longer. Add wine and bring to a boil, stirring frequently. Return chicken to the skillet, reduce heat to low, cover tightly, and cook approximately 20 minutes, or until juices run clear when a thigh is pricked with a sharp knife point. Turn chicken once or twice during cooking.

Remove finished chicken to a heated platter and keep warm while you finish the sauce. Reduce the cooking liquid over medium heat until nicely thickened. Adjust seasonings.

Pour the sauce over the warm chicken, sprinkle with minced chives, and garnish with watercress sprigs.

AFTERTHOUGHT: You may wish to crisp the chicken skin under a hot broiler just before saucing.

CHICKEN STUFFED WITH BRUSCHETTA

Serves six

This is a dish to nourish the soul; let those who will murmur of bean sprouts, tofu, and unsaturated fats.

1 roasting chicken, about 5
   pounds
Salt
Freshly ground black pepper
6 slices sourdough French bread,
   about ½-inch thick
2–3 garlic cloves, peeled
3 tablespoons fruity olive oil
2 teaspoons mixed dried herbs
   (oregano, thyme, and sage)
Handful of chopped fresh parsley
1 small piece salt fatback
   (parboiled 3 minutes, drained,
   and sliced thin)

2–3 tablespoons rendered chicken
   fat (page 173) or butter
1 medium onion, chopped
1 leek, white part only, sliced
   thin
2 sprigs parsley
2 bunches scallions, trimmed,
   leaving 2 inches of green top
1 cup chicken broth or water
Watercress sprigs

Preheat oven to 425°F. Place oven rack on lower shelf.

Remove all fat from chicken and reserve. Trim and reserve liver and heart. Chop gizzard into small pieces. Wipe cavity with damp paper towels and season with salt and pepper.

Toast sourdough slices and rub with garlic cloves, reserving remaining garlic. Sprinkle with olive oil and 1 1/2 teaspoons of dried herb mixture. Tear into large pieces into a bowl and combine with chopped parsley, a few grindings of pepper, and remaining coarsely chopped cloves of garlic. Stuff cavity with bread mixture and then liver and heart. Truss chicken loosely. Pat dry with paper towels, cover breast with fatback slices, and tie in place. Pat remaining 1/2 teaspoon of dried herbs onto chicken.

Melt poultry fat or butter over low heat in a heavy casserole large enough to hold chicken comfortably. Add onion, leek, and parsley sprigs, and cook until softened, about 5 minutes. Add chopped gizzard and combine.

Roll chicken around in vegetable mixture to coat evenly, leaving it breast side down. Transfer to preheated oven and roast, uncovered, 15 minutes.

Reduce temperature to 350°F and turn chicken onto one side. Cover casserole with buttered aluminum foil, and then with its lid, and roast 20 minutes. Turn chicken on its other side. Scatter scallions around chicken and baste with juices. Re-cover and roast an additional 20 minutes.

Turn chicken breast side up. Remove fatback slices, and continue roasting approximately 20 minutes more, basting scallions and chicken occasionally. When the thickest part of the thigh is pierced with a fork and the juices run clear, the chicken is done.

Remove chicken and scallions and keep warm. Strain roasting juices into a stainless-steel bowl and set into another, larger bowl filled with ice water. Discard solids.

Deglaze pan with a cup of chicken broth or water, bring to a boil, and scrape up all browned bits. Turn off heat. Meanwhile, remove and discard the fat from the cooking juices, which will have congealed. Add defatted juices to the pot and bring to a boil, reducing liquid to about 1 1/4 cups. Adjust seasonings and keep warm.

Transfer chicken to a heated serving platter. Discard strings and spoon stuffing from cavity onto platter. Surround chicken with scallions. Spoon juices over stuffing until saturated. Garnish with watercress sprigs and serve. Carve chicken at the table and pass remaining sauce.

BREAST OF CHICKEN WITH GARLIC STUFFING

Serves six

Go ahead, make this chicken and its sauce; it's a fine dish. Or—slice the finished chicken, cut some soft French rolls in half and dip them in vinaigrette, lay on the chicken slices (don't skimp), press the rolls together and wrap them in foil. Now, get a bottle of wine and a friend, and go on a picnic—it's good for your soul.

3 whole chicken breasts, boned, skinned, and halved
3–4 tablespoons light olive oil
1 small onion, minced
2 heads garlic, separated into cloves, blanched, peeled and minced

2 ounces prosciutto, minced
1 teaspoon chopped fresh herbs (oregano, thyme, or sage) or ½ teaspoon dried
½ cup minced fresh parsley
½ cup grated Parmesan cheese
½ cup fresh bread crumbs

Salt
Freshly ground black pepper
Flour
2 tablespoons butter
1 cup chicken broth

½ cup plus a dash of dry white
  wine
½ cup cream
Watercress leaves or minced fresh
  parsley

Flatten chicken breasts between two sheets of plastic wrap by smacking them with the bottom of a small heavy skillet or pot. Remove them to a platter, cover, and reserve while you make the stuffing.

Heat 2 tablespoons of the olive oil in a large skillet, add the onion, and cook 1 minute. Add garlic and prosciutto and cook until lightly browned, 3 to 4 minutes. Remove from heat and cool slightly.

Add oregano, parsley, cheese, bread crumbs, salt to taste, and a grinding or two of pepper; mix well. Add just enough remaining olive oil to moisten the mixture.

Divide the stuffing into 6 portions and spread it evenly over each chicken piece. Roll each one up, tucking the edges in as you roll, and tie them with string or secure with toothpicks. Dust them lightly with flour.

Heat butter in a heavy skillet over moderate heat until it is bubbling. Add chicken rolls and cook them, turning once or twice, until they are a light golden brown. Lower heat, add 1/2 cup chicken broth and a dash of wine, cover, and simmer until tender, 10 to 15 minutes. The juices should run clear when pierced. Don't overdo this step; we want them just cooked through. Transfer the finished chicken to a serving dish, remove toothpicks or strings, and keep them warm while you run up a little sauce.

Turn up the heat and add the remaining broth and wine, scraping all the brown bits into the liquid as you stir. When the broth has reduced to about 1/2 cup, blend in the cream and cook over medium heat until the sauce has thickened nicely and reduced to about 3/4 cup. Taste for seasonings. Pour the sauce over the chicken rolls, garnish with watercress leaves or minced parsley, and serve them forth.

❧

THAI GARLIC SHRIMP

Serves four

Guaranteed to please the deepest-dyed garlic fan. It'll knock your socks off!

Roots and 1 inch of stems from
* 2 bunches cilantro*
1 large head garlic, separated
* into cloves and peeled*
¼ cup vegetable oil
½ teaspoon freshly ground black
* pepper*
1 pound raw shrimp, peeled and
* deveined*

1 cup water
3 tablespoons Thai fish sauce
* (nam pla; see Afterthought)*
1½ tablespoons sugar
Thin cucumber slices
Radish slices
Cilantro sprigs with leaves

Finely mince cilantro and garlic in a blender or food processor or crush in a mortar with a pestle until a paste is formed.

Heat oil in a heavy skillet or wok over medium-high heat. Add cilantro–garlic mixture and pepper and stir-fry until garlic is golden brown.

Add shrimp and toss several seconds until coated with mixture. Add water, fish sauce, and sugar and bring to a boil. Lower heat and cook slowly 2 minutes, or until shrimp are just cooked through.

Transfer to a heated serving dish. Garnish with cucumber and radish slices and cilantro sprigs, and serve immediately. Traditionally served with hot rice.

AFTERTHOUGHT: Nam pla is to Thai cooking what soy sauce is to the Chinese and Japanese. It is sold in bottles in Oriental markets and many supermarkets.

❧

BRANDADE

Serves six

A jewel of French country cooking. Sturdy and reliable, it may be served warm or cold.

1½ pounds dried salt cod
1 onion, grated
3 garlic cloves, peeled
1 large potato, boiled and
  quartered
1 cup half-and-half, at room
  temperature

1 cup olive oil
Juice of 1 lemon
Freshly ground black pepper
Freshly grated nutmeg

Soak the cod overnight in a large basin of cold water, changing the water four or five times. Drain. Taste a bit of fish to see if it has desalted enough and gained a fresh, fishlike texture. If not, continue soaking a bit longer.

After the cod has been properly soaked, remove the skin and bones, and place it in a pan of cold water. Add the grated onion and bring to a boil. As the water begins to boil, remove the pan from the heat and let it cool. Drain and set aside.

Purée the garlic with fork tines. Flake the fish with your fingers into a large mixing bowl. Add the garlic purée and the potato. Beat the mixture, adding the cream and oil alternately, bit by bit, until the mixture resembles fluffy whipped potatoes. When all the cream and oil are incorporated and the mixture is quite smooth, add the lemon juice, pepper, and nutmeg. Blend again. Taste for salt (which it probably won't need).

To serve warm: Reheat the brandade over a low flame, stirring continuously. Serve surrounded by triangles of bread sautéed in olive oil. Garnish with watercress sprigs and black olives. A tart salad would be a good accompaniment.

To serve cold: Chill and mound in tomato shells or on lettuce leaves accompanied by hard-boiled eggs and fresh basil garnish.

AFTERTHOUGHTS: When you buy the salt cod, choose the center pieces. The tails are inclined to be thin, scraggly, and quite bony.

Brandade may also be used as a delicious omelet filling.

GRILLED LAMB WITH LEMON-ANCHOVY MARINADE

Serves six to eight

I like to cook this in the summer when fennel grows profusely, and throw some of their feathery leaves on the fire for the smoky, aromatic flavor. Springs of rosemary work also.

3 garlic cloves, peeled

2 tablespoons anchovy paste

2 tablespoons fennel seed

½ lemon, sliced thin

Freshly ground black pepper

Handful of parsley leaves

⅓ cup olive oil

Juice of 1 large lemon

3 pounds boned lamb (leg or shoulder) cut into 1½-inch cubes

2–3 onions, sliced into ½-inch wedges

Put the garlic, anchovy paste, fennel, lemon slices, pepper, and parsley in a food processor and process with quick on/off turns until the lemon peel resembles rice grains. Add the olive oil and lemon juice and blend just long enough to incorporate.

Place lamb cubes in a heavy plastic bag (or double bag) large enough to hold it comfortably. Pour in marinade, seal bag, and turn over several times until lamb is evenly coated with the mixture. Marinate 2 hours at room temperature, or 4–6 hours, refrigerated (or even overnight), turning bag occasionally.

A half hour before grilling, soak bamboo skewers in water to prevent burning.

Skewer lamb and onion wedges alternately, and grill over hot coals, basting with marinade as they cook, until lamb is nicely browned but pink inside. This will vary, depending on the heat of the coals, and the distance grill is above the heat source, but begin to check after 5–7 minutes on each side. Serve immediately when done.

AFTERTHOUGHTS: Serve with Red Onion Flowers (page 122) and Roman Potatoes (page 47), or with skewers of grilled vegetables (yellow and green squashes, red peppers, baby eggplants, tiny onions, cherry tomatoes, etc., that have been lightly oiled before cooking).

LEG OF LAMB WITH GARLIC SAUCE
(Gigot d'Agneau à l'Aillade)

Serves six

In English or French, a dish to gladden the hearts of garlic fanatics. For a truly French accent, the lamb should be cooked just until a tender pink.

1 leg of lamb, about 5 pounds
4 garlic cloves, slivered
2 teaspoons herbes de Provence,
  or 1 teaspoon each dried
  thyme and rosemary
Coarse salt
Freshly ground black pepper

3 tablespoons peanut oil
½ cup dry white wine
½ cup chicken broth
1 head garlic, separated into
  cloves, unpeeled
Fresh mint leaves

Trim off excess fat and tough outer skin from lamb, leaving a thin layer of fat. Make slits all over the lamb and insert a sliver of garlic into each incision. Rub the meat with herbs, salt, and pepper, and then with peanut oil, massaging oil into meat. Let stand for 1 to 2 hours at room temperature.

Preheat oven to 425°F.

Place meat fat side up on a rack in a roasting pan. Set pan on upper-middle oven shelf and roast for 20 minutes. Reduce heat to 350°F. Pour wine and broth into bottom of roaster and scatter in the unpeeled garlic cloves. Cook for another 40 to 45 minutes for medium-rare (135° to 140°F on a meat thermometer). Baste occasionally, adding more wine or stock as needed so pan does not cook dry.

When done to your taste, remove lamb from oven. With a slotted spoon, remove garlic cloves and set aside.

Add enough broth or wine to bring liquid content of pan to

1 1/2 cups. Place over direct heat and bring to a boil, scraping up any browned bits. Reduce to about 1 cup. Taste for seasonings and adjust as necessary. Turn off heat and skim off any excess fat.

Pinch cooled garlic cloves out of their skins into a shallow bowl. Mash lightly with a fork and add to sauce, stirring to combine. Reheat sauce briefly and keep warm.

Slice lamb and arrange on a heated serving platter. Sprinkle lightly with freshly ground pepper and garnish with a few fresh mint leaves. Serve with garlic sauce.

RACK OF LAMB WITH MUSTARD CRUST AND GARLIC-GINGER CONSERVE

Serves eight

The unexpected flavor and texture of Garlic-Ginger Conserve adds a flourish to this delectable lamb.

½ cup dry bread crumbs	*Salt*
3 tablespoons butter, softened	*Freshly ground black pepper*
1 tablespoon chopped fresh	*3 tablespoons olive oil*
tarragon	*2 tablespoons Dijon mustard*
2 racks of lamb with 10 ribs	*Watercress sprigs*
each, trimmed to expose 2	*Garlic-Ginger Conserve (recipe*
inches of rib bone	*follows)*

Preheat oven to 450°F.

Combine bread crumbs, butter, and tarragon in a small bowl.

Sprinkle lamb on all sides with salt and pepper, and then brush with olive oil. Cover exposed rib bones with aluminum foil to prevent burning. Place lamb on rack in roasting pan and roast 10 minutes. Remove from oven and reduce heat to 350°.

Brush lamb with mustard, then with bread crumb mixture. Return to oven and roast about 30 minutes for medium-rare. Let stand 10 minutes before carving.

Place racks on serving platter and garnish with watercress sprigs. Carve at the table, slicing between ribs with a sharp knife. Pass Garlic-Ginger Conserve.

GARLIC-GINGER CONSERVE

About 1 1/2 cups

1 pound fresh garlic cloves,
  coarsely chopped, about 2½
  cups
½–⅔ cup sugar

½ cup water
1 tablespoon grated fresh ginger
1 tablespoon currants
Few gratings of fresh lemon peel

Combine garlic, sugar, and water in a heavy saucepan. Bring to a boil over high heat, stirring constantly.

When mixture boils, reduce heat to very low and add ginger. Simmer, stirring occasionally, until garlic is soft and mixture is light, golden, and slightly syrupy, about 20 minutes. Add currants and lemon peel the last 5 minutes of simmering.

Spoon into a small bowl and allow to cool to room temperature. Refrigerate, covered, up to one week. Serve at room temperature.

GARLIC BEEF RAGOUT

Serves four

While this lusty stew simmers away, you'll have plenty of time to do whatever pleases you most; in fact, it will be even more succulent if you cook it the day before. Steamed young red potatoes dusted with plenty of chopped parsley, and some crisp broccoli florets are the perfect complement.

2½ pounds boneless lean beef
  chuck
1 tablespoon cornstarch
2 tablespoons vegetable oil
1 cup dry red wine
2 cups beef broth
1 large head garlic, separated
  into cloves, unpeeled
1 bay leaf

Small handful of fresh thyme
  and/or rosemary
or
1 teaspoon dried thyme and/or
  rosemary
Salt
Freshly ground black pepper
2 tablespoons finely minced fresh
  parsley

Dry beef with paper towels and cut into 1 1/2-inch chunks. Toss with 1 tablespoon cornstarch until evenly coated. Heat oil in a heavy casserole over medium-high heat and brown beef in small batches, transferring them with tongs to a bowl as they are browned.

Preheat oven to 300°F.

Pour off fat from casserole and add red wine. Deglaze casserole, scraping up any brown bits that cling to the bottom and sides. Reduce liquid by half.

Add the beef and any accumulated juices, the broth, garlic cloves, herbs, and salt and pepper to taste. Bring liquid to a boil. Cover and transfer casserole to the preheated oven. Braise the beef for 1 1/2 hours, or until the meat is tender when pierced with a fork. Check occasionally to make sure liquid does not cook away; add broth or wine as necessary.

Remove meat with a slotted spoon and set aside. Purée cooking liquid and garlic through the fine disk of a food mill into a bowl, or run through a blender. Return the meat and puréed sauce to the casserole and heat the mixture over low heat, stirring occasionally, until heated through. Transfer stew to a heated serving dish, sprinkle with finely minced fresh parsley, and serve.

ORANGE-GARLIC BEEF

Serves six

A delicious concoction of tender stir-fried beef scented with orange and spicy with garlic and brave red chilies. It may be assembled in advance or put together in a flash while the rice cooks. I usually serve the beef in individual portions, surrounding a mold of Japanese rice (see Afterthoughts), and garnished with a few thinly sliced bright green scallion tops.

*2½ pounds boneless lean beef
    chuck*

MARINADE
2 tablespoons soy sauce
*2 tablespoons medium-dry sherry
    or mirin (sweet rice wine)*

1½ tablespoons cornstarch
1 tablespoon water
*2 teaspoons peeled and grated
    fresh ginger*
*1½ teaspoons Oriental toasted
    sesame oil*
1 tablespoon finely minced garlic

ASSEMBLY

½ cup shredded orange peel

2–3 dried hot chili peppers

½ cup water

¼ cup soy sauce

3 tablespoons medium-dry sherry or mirin (sweet rice wine)

2 teaspoons cornstarch

1 teaspoon sugar

1½ teaspoons Oriental toasted sesame oil

Freshly ground black pepper to taste

½ cup plus 2 tablespoons peanut oil

Cut beef crosswise into 1/2-inch-thick slices, then cut the slices across the grain into 2-by-1/4-inch strips.

In a large bowl combine marinade ingredients. Add the beef and toss to combine. Marinate, covered, 2 hours at room temperature, or overnight in the refrigerator.

Blanch the shredded orange peel in boiling water for 1 minute and drain thoroughly. Reserve.

Tear chilies in half and discard seeds, then tear into 1/2-inch pieces. Set aside. Wash hands carefully after handling the chilies.

In a small bowl combine the water, soy sauce, sherry, cornstarch, sugar, and sesame oil. Add pepper to taste. Drain the beef through a large sieve set over the soy sauce mixture. Return the beef to the large bowl, and add to it 1 tablespoon of peanut oil, stirring until meat is well-coated with oil.

Heat a wok or large heavy skillet over high heat until hot, add 1/2 cup peanut oil, and heat to smoking. Stir-fry the beef in two batches, about 1 minute per batch, or until the meat is no longer pink. Do not overcook. Remove with a slotted spoon and set aside in a bowl. Pour off fat remaining in the pan and wipe clean with paper towels.

Reheat the wok over high heat until it is hot and add remaining tablespoon of peanut oil, heating until hot. Add orange rind and chili peppers and stir-fry until fragrant, 5 to 10 seconds. Stir soy sauce mixture once again and add to wok, standing back to avoid inhaling chili steam. Bring mixture to a boil, stirring constantly. Add the beef and toss a minute or two, or until the sauce has thickened and the beef is thoroughly heated. Transfer the beef mixture to a heated serving dish and serve immediately.

AFTERTHOUGHTS: Japanese rice is essential because it will stick together and that's what we're after. Besides that, I love the taste of it. Blue Rose is my favorite, and is usually available in supermarkets.

To prepare the rice, simply cook it according to package directions. When it's tender, rinse a custard cup with cold water, pack it with the hot rice, turn it out on the heated serving plate, and there you are with a pretty white mound to surround with the spicy beef and its sauce.

CALF'S LIVER WITH JUNIPER AND GARLIC

Serves six

A dish with a charming French accent.

6 slices calf's liver, each ⅓ inch
    thick
2 teaspoons juniper berries,
    crushed
Salt
Freshly ground black pepper
6 thin slices bacon

1 tablespoon each peanut oil and
    olive oil
6–12 garlic cloves, peeled (12
    may not be enough!)
Splash of apple cider vinegar
Squeeze of lemon

Dry the liver with paper towels. Sprinkle with crushed juniper berries and salt and pepper to taste.

Roll up each slice and wrap with bacon. Secure with string.

Heat the oils in a heavy-bottomed skillet. Add the liver rolls and garlic and sauté for 2 minutes. Turn the rolls and lower the flame. Add a splash of apple cider vinegar, swirling it in the pan to blend, and continue to cook for 25 minutes, turning the rolls occasionally.

Remove rolls and garlic cloves to a heated platter. Snip and remove strings. Keep rolls warm while you finish the sauce.

Spoon out excess bacon fat. Turn up the heat under the pan and, whisking constantly, add a healthy squeeze of lemon as you incorporate all pan juices. Turn off heat and drizzle a bit of sauce over each roll. Serve at once.

AFTERTHOUGHT: Serve this with Red Onion Marmalade (page 135), small steamed red potatoes, and a salad of young spinach leaves, thinly sliced red apple, chopped scallions, and a mango–chutney vinaigrette. A dessert of spiced pears would be nice.

YIN-YANG PORK

Serves four to six

I made this one just to suit myself, and I think you'll like it, too. I could pull out some trusty adjectives and run them by you, but why don't you take my word for it? It's wonderful.

2½ pounds trimmed boneless
   pork shoulder, cut into
   1½-inch pieces
2 tablespoons peanut oil
1 cup dry red wine
1 large head garlic, separated
   into cloves, blanched, and
   peeled .
1 cup beef broth, homemade or
   canned
2 tablespoons Chinese sweetened
   black vinegar (see
   Afterthought)

2 tablespoons ketchup
Grated peel of 1 medium orange
1–2 small dried red chilies
4 thin slices fresh ginger,
   unpeeled
¼ cup light soy sauce
1 tablespoon cornstarch
Pineapple Garnish (recipe
   follows)

Pat the pork dry with paper towels. Heat oil in a heavy casserole over a fairly high flame. Brown the meat in two batches, tossing frequently. Remove meat to a plate as it finishes. When all the meat is cooked, discard fat. Pour in red wine and deglaze the pan, scraping up any brown bits. Reduce the wine to 1/2 cup.

Return the pork and any accumulated juices to the pot. Add the garlic cloves, beef broth, vinegar, ketchup, orange peel, chilies, and ginger slices and simmer over low heat, covered, until the meat is tender when pierced with a fork, about 11/2 hours. Stir occasionally to keep from sticking.

Remove the pork to a bowl while you finish the sauce. Discard chilies and ginger slices. Pour the sauce through a strainer, mashing the garlic cloves through with the back of a spoon.

Combine soy sauce and cornstarch and add to sauce, stirring well. Return the pork to the pan and simmer just until sauce has thickened a bit and the meat is heated through. Serve garnished with sautéed fresh pineapple.

AFTERTHOUGHT: Chinese sweetened black vinegar is as precious a liquid as balsamic vinegar or, perhaps, Joy perfume. You should be able to find it in any Oriental market. If not, a fairly close substitute may be made by combining 2 tablespoons sherry wine vinegar with 1/2 teaspoon sugar and a pinch of Chinese five-spice powder (in most grocery stores) or, failing that, a pinch of ground cloves.

PINEAPPLE GARNISH

Cut a fresh pineapple into as many rings, slices, or spears as you think you'll need, remembering that thinner slices take less time to sauté. Lay them on a paper towel until you're ready for them. Place a tablespoon of butter in a large skillet over moderate heat. When the foam subsides, add the pineapple slices and sauté them until nicely browned on both sides, approximately 3 minutes a side. Serve warm.

WEST INDIAN ROAST PORK

Serves six to eight

Straight from the West Indies, this glorious roast is fragrant with garlic and spices. With its satiny, sweet-tart sauce, it's a most festive dish and worthy becoming one of your favorites. Served with roasted slices of red yams and thick ovals of plantain sautéed with a dash of lime and a sprinkle of brown sugar, it's hard to beat. When my friend, author James Wohl, told me to get some sex into the book, I served this and told him it was as close as I could get. He ate it—and agreed!

1 center-cut pork loin, about 5
  pounds, with its bones
4–6 garlic cloves, slivered
  lengthwise
12–14 slivers of fresh ginger
½ teaspoon ground cloves
Salt
Freshly ground pepper

½ cup dark rum
½ cup brown sugar
1 teaspoon ground ginger
2 cups chicken broth
Juice and grated peel of 1 lime
1 tablespoon cornstarch mixed
  with ¼ cup water

Preheat oven to 450°F.

Score the fat side of the loin in a diamond pattern at 1-inch intervals, about 1/2 inch deep. Poke small holes all over the surface of the loin with the tip of a sharp knife and insert garlic and ginger slivers in each hole. Rub the meat with ground cloves.

Sprinkle meat with salt and pepper. Place the pork on a rack in a roasting pan and then into the preheated oven for 30 minutes. Reduce heat to 325° and continue roasting for another 30 minutes.

Blend 3 or 4 tablespoons of the rum with the brown sugar and ground ginger. Set aside.

After 1 hour, remove the roast from the oven, leaving heat on. Transfer roast to a platter. Deglaze the pan with the chicken broth, scraping up brown particles. Rub the meat with the brown sugar mixture, place it back in the pan, and return to the oven for another 45 minutes.

When the roast is done, remove it from the oven and allow it to rest while you finish the sauce.

Pour the liquid from the roasting pan into a saucepan. Add the remaining rum, lime juice, and peel. Bring the sauce to a boil and add the cornstarch mixture. Stir and cook the sauce until thickened. Correct seasonings.

Slice the pork and arrange the slices on a heated serving platter. Drizzle with a couple of spoonfuls of sauce and serve. Pass remaining sauce.

> . . . a good meal in troubled times is always that
> much salvaged from disaster.
> —A. J. Liebling

PORK WITH ORANGE JUICE AND CILANTRO

Serves four to six

Mr. Liebling was always one of my major heros. A trencherman of epic proportions and eclectic tastes, he wrote with grace and style about prize fighters, beautiful women, and food; took serious matters lightly and lighter matters with wit and amiable concern. A better companion cannot be found. I like to think that this dish, richly aromatic and abundant, would have met with his approval—in palmy days or troubled ones. A toast to A.J.!

2½–3 pounds whole pork
   tenderloins, trimmed of most
   fat
5 large garlic cloves, sliced
   lengthwise into quarters
¼ teaspoon ground allspice
¼ teaspoon ground cloves
Salt
Freshly ground black pepper
⅓ cup cilantro stems
1½ cups chicken broth

10 juniper berries, crushed
1 tablespoon butter
4 scallions, finely chopped
Juice of 2 small limes
½ teaspoon dry mustard
Juice of 2 large oranges
1 pickled jalapeño pepper,
   minced
¼ cup torn cilantro leaves
Paper-thin orange slices, halved

Preheat oven to 400°F.

Make 20 incisions all over the pork with the point of a very sharp knife and insert garlic slices. Rub the meat with allspice and cloves and season to taste with salt and pepper. Place in a roasting pan and sprinkle the top with coriander stems. Pour in the broth and scatter the juniper berries around the meat.

Cook the meat in the preheated oven until tender, about 40 minutes. Remove from oven and transfer the tenderloins to a heated serving platter. Cover loosely with foil and keep warm in the turned-off oven with door ajar.

Skim as much fat as possible from the pan broth, reserving 1 tablespoon. Melt the butter over moderate heat in a small saucepan. Add the skimmed tablespoon of fat, the scallions, and 1 tablespoon of the lime juice. Sauté until soft. Pour in the remaining lime juice and strained pan liquid (including any brown bits). Add the mustard, orange juice, and minced pepper, and cook, uncovered, for 3 or 4 minutes. Drop in the cilantro leaves, stir, and keep warm.

Slice the meat and arrange in attractive, overlapping slices. Spoon some of the sauce over the meat, and garnish with orange slices. Serve immediately and pass a bowl of the remaining sauce.

VEGETABLES

ROMAN POTATOES

What we have here is a celebration of mighty garlic and tender red potatoes. Slowly sautéed in fine olive oil (the operative word here is *slowly*), the potatoes are crisp and gilded and the rowdy garlic soft and mellow. I grow rosemary in my garden and use it lavishly. In any case, fresh rosemary is essential; the dry stuff just won't do.

This is a decent recipe, but after you do it once you'll probably want to use more garlic. It's so good treated this way that there's almost never enough to please everyone.

2 medium red potatoes per person
Olive oil for sauté
2 large whole peeled garlic cloves
  per person

2–3 fresh rosemary sprigs, about
  4–5 inches long
Coarse salt
Freshly ground black pepper

Scrub and dry the potatoes, cut them in half, then in quarters the long way.

In a large sauté pan (nonstick is a boon here), heat enough oil to cover the bottom generously. When the oil is hot (but not smoking), add the potatoes and sauté them slowly over a medium-low fire. After about 5 minutes, add the garlic cloves and rosemary, and continue to sauté slowly, shaking the pan now and then, and turning the potatoes as necessary. Watch the garlic carefully so it doesn't burn.

When the potatoes are beautifully browned and crisp, they are probably done. Season with salt and a few grindings of pepper and serve immediately.

GARLIC SCALLOPED POTATOES

Serves 8 generously

Whoopee!

3 pounds yellow potatoes	*Freshly ground black pepper*
2 garlic cloves	*6 tablespoons butter*
Salt	*1½ pints heavy cream*

Preheat oven to 325°F.

Peel one potato at a time and slice thinly, dropping slices into a bowl of cold water to keep them from darkening. When all potatoes have been sliced, drain and pat dry in a towel. Keep them wrapped in the towel as you continue.

Rub a shallow earthenware dish with garlic cloves until the cloves practically disappear. Butter dish well.

Arrange a layer of potatoes, season with salt and pepper, and dot with butter. Continue layering in this manner until all potatoes are used, increasing the butter if necessary. Pour cream over the potatoes and dot with more butter.

Bake about 1 1/2 hours. (Do not try to cook the potatoes at a higher temperature or the cream will curdle before it is absorbed.) During the last 10 minutes, raise the heat to 400°F to brown the top. Serve from the casserole.

CARAMELIZED GARLIC

You will find many, many uses for these pearls—soups, ragouts, with sautéed vegetables, as accompaniments to grilled or roasted meats or poultry; and the same recipe works well with tiny onions, too.

2 heads garlic (preferably with large cloves), cloves separated and unpeeled

2 teaspoons butter
1½–2 teaspoons sugar

Preheat oven to 250°F.

Drop garlic cloves into a small saucepan of boiling water for 2 minutes. Drain, cool under cold running water, and drain again. Peel off skins.

Melt butter in a heavy ovenproof pan. Add garlic, sprinkle with sugar, and place in preheated oven. Bake, uncovered, about 1 hour, until garlic is very soft and golden. Do not let garlic brown; adjust heat if necessary, and shake pan two or three times during baking.

AFTERTHOUGHT: If you bake garlic longer, say another 45 minutes or so, until they are very soft, you may use them blended into sauces and spreads.

ROASTED EGGPLANTS

These roasted beauties have a great variety of uses: as part of an antipasto tray, as the basis for caponata, with pasta, or as an accompaniment to grilled meats or poultry. This is a wizard way to do eggplant and a welcome change from the ubiquitous ratatouille.

If you cannot locate pretty little Japanese eggplants, buy the smallest, most perfect ones you can find, and do this to them:

Take 2 or 3 slices bacon, cut into 1/4-inch pieces, and roll them in a mixture of dried herbs (oregano, rosemary, sage, thyme, whatever you like). Cut some peeled garlic cloves into lengthwise slices.

Now cut slashes in 8 or 10 Japanese eggplants about 1/2 inch deep, and stuff each slash with the bacon and garlic. Rub the eggplants all over with olive oil and place them on a cookie sheet in a hot oven (about 375°F) until they are soft, about 30 minutes. Now then, you're ready to eat them, warm or cold, as part of an antipasto, or as an accompaniment to an entrée.

STIR-FRIED SPINACH WITH GARLIC

Serves four

A beautiful, brilliant green accompaniment to fish, poultry, and pork dishes.

2 pounds very young spinach
2 tablespoons olive oil

1 or 2 garlic cloves, finely
minced
Tamari or soy sauce to taste

Wash spinach carefully, taking care to remove every trace of grit. Dry. Trim ends, but do not remove stems if young spinach. (Young chard also works well in this dish.)

Heat olive oil in large skillet or wok until hot. Stir-fry garlic 30 seconds or less, just until a pale golden blond. Add spinach and toss gently, cooking until wilted, tender, and bright green. Remove from heat.

Drizzle with soy sauce to taste and serve immediately.

ROASTED TOMATOES

An excellent accompaniment for any roast or grilled meat. Be certain to save the roasting juices; your guests will want to sop it all up with the good bread you serve. And another word of advice: make a little sauce with these for pasta; you'll wonder how you ever did anything else. If you have any tomatoes left over, which is unlikely, they make a divine filling for omelets.

To make them is simplicity itself; here's how:

Preheat the oven to 350°F. Take 8 big, red ripe tomatoes (this recipe works almost as well with tomatoes that are not so well-flavored; the baking renders them delicious). Cut a slice from the stem end just below the scar and gently squeeze out most of the juice. Place them cut side up on a shallow baking pan (nonaluminum) that you have oiled. Now, with a paring knife, cut a large X across the top of each one, about 1/2 inch deep, being mindful not to cut all the way through. Scatter 3 finely minced garlic cloves evenly over them, and *liberally* drizzle them with good olive oil. Season with salt and pepper to taste and bake them in the preheated oven until they have collapsed, are a rich, dark red, and the garlic is glazed and tender, about 45 minutes. Remove them from the heat and allow to cool to room temperature before you serve them.

If you choose to use the tomatoes for pasta, simply cut each one into quarters and scrape the tomatoes and their juice onto the hot pasta. There you have the basis for a perfect little sauce. Just add more olive oil and salt, a squeeze of lemon, and a handful of fresh herbs.

LIMA BEANS SAUTÉED WITH GARLIC

Serves six

1 pound fresh young lima beans
or
2 boxes (10 ounces each) frozen
  baby lima beans
4–5 tablespoons olive oil
1½ tablespoons finely minced
  garlic

Salt
Freshly ground black pepper
½ cup day-old bread crumbs,
  lightly toasted
2 tablespoons finely minced fresh
  parsley

Wash and dry fresh beans, or blanch, drain, and dry frozen ones.

Heat the oil in a large skillet and sauté garlic until a pale golden blond. Do not let garlic darken. Add lima beans, salt, and pepper, and sauté until beans are heated thoroughly. Add bread crumbs and toss lightly with the beans until they are well-coated with the crumbs.

Serve at once sprinkled with finely minced parsley.

AFTERTHOUGHT: This recipe also works well with green beans, Italian green beans, yard-long beans, or Swiss chard (slice ribs in thin diagonals, blanch a minute or two, drain; add coarsely chopped leaves toward the end of cooking time for the stems). Proceed as above.

SALADS AND DRESSINGS

MUSTARD VINAIGRETTE

About 1 cup

This is a perfect vinaigrette and one of the first things I teach my students.

1 garlic clove, peeled
½ teaspoon salt
2 tablespoons Dijon mustard
3 tablespoons sherry wine
*　vinegar*

1 cup oil, half olive, half peanut
1 egg yolk
½ teaspoon chopped fresh
*　tarragon, or a pinch of dried*

Mash garlic with salt. Add mustard and vinegar and blend well.

Add oil in a thin stream, whisking constantly. When an emulsion has formed, whisk in the egg yolk and tarragon.

VARIATIONS

*Leave out the egg yolk if you are feeling virtuous and want a lighter dressing.

*Chop a handful of fresh parsley, watercress leaves, and any fresh herbs (by hand or in the blender) and stir into the dressing for a nice green treat.

*A very acceptable dressing for a primo Caesar salad may be made with the basic Mustard Vinaigrette by stirring in a couple of tablespoons or more of anchovy paste (depending on your passion for anchovies), along with enough Worcestershire to make the salad sing. The anchovy paste combines with the dressing with some finesse, but there are those who don't fancy anchovies, poor darlings. Finish your salad with a squirt or two of fresh lemon, plenty of garlic croutons, and generous amounts of fine, freshly grated Romano or Parmesan cheese. (By the way, Crosse & Blackwell's anchovy sauce is even better than paste in this dressing, or any other sauce that needs a little kick, a little mystery.)

*The basic vinaigrette with a handful of coarsely chopped shallots along with fresh parsley is splendid spooned over sliced ripe avocados.

*While on the subject of shallots, make a vinaigrette with lime juice, a bland oil, shallots, and honey. Stir in half of a very ripe fresh mango and serve with fruit or chicken salad.

*Stir nice big chunks of blue cheese or Roquefort into the basic vinaigrette, but don't mash them up—allow their presence to be known. Scatter 1/2 cup of coarsely chopped toasted walnuts over the greens, and, for a prodigal treat, crisp bacon as well. Wouldn't that be good over lightly cooked, chilled green beans?

*For creamy vinaigrette, add a tablespoon or so of heavy cream when finishing the dressing. Good with cold asparagus or chilled butter lettuce.

*If you have a tablespoon of leftover Concasse (page 17), add it to the basic vinaigrette. Wonderful with antipasto salad.

AFTERTHOUGHT: Make only enough dressing to use immediately. Vinaigrettes do not really improve with age.

BROCCOLI SALAD
WITH CREAMY GARLIC SAUCE

Serves eight

This sauce is not only divine on cold broccoli, it's wonderful on fish and sandwiches, and you'll think of plenty of other ways to use it once you taste it.

2 bunches young broccoli
2 teaspoons salt
2 garlic cloves, unpeeled
Creamy Garlic Sauce (recipe
* follows)*

Rolled anchovy fillets stuffed with
* capers*

Separate broccoli into florets. Discard toughened stem ends; thinly slice tender stems.

Add salt and garlic cloves to a gallon of water and bring to a boil. Add broccoli and blanch for 1 1/2 to 2 minutes. Drain in a colander and place under cold running water to cool. Discard garlic cloves. Drain broccoli thoroughly and pat dry with paper towels. Chill.

Just before serving, toss broccoli with enough sauce to lightly coat. Garnish with rolled anchovy fillets stuffed with capers.

CREAMY GARLIC SAUCE

About 1 cup

1 cup fresh mayonnaise
1 tablespoon roasted garlic purée
* (see Afterthoughts)*
1 tablespoon fresh lemon juice
1 teaspoon anchovy paste
3 tablespoons freshly grated
* Parmesan cheese*

¼–½ teaspoon tarragon, dried
* or fresh*
Dash of Tabasco
2 tablespoons heavy cream

Place all ingredients but the cream in a small bowl and blend thoroughly. Add the cream and blend again.

AFTERTHOUGHTS: Use this sauce with any cooked, cold vegetable. Mix with leftover cooked, cold fish or tuna and serve with toast triangles, or as a filling for sandwiches. Spread the sauce on fish before broiling. Wow!

To make roasted garlic purée: Rub 4–6 unpeeled garlic cloves in your hands with a little olive oil. Place them in a small baking tin and roast them at 350°F for about 1 hour. (Do this when you are using your oven for other dishes). After about 20 minutes the garlic will have colored lightly. Add a little water and baste or shake the pan frequently while they roast. When soft, set them aside to cool.

When you can handle them comfortably, pinch the clove out of its skin and mash lightly with a fork.

GARLIC MINT DRESSING

About 1/2 cup

An aromatic dressing, freshened with lime and mint.

1 garlic clove, finely minced
2 tablespoons fresh lime juice
1 teaspoon Dijon mustard
5–6 fresh mint leaves, finely
chopped

⅛ teaspoon sugar
¼ teaspoon salt (or to taste)
Freshly ground black pepper
⅓ cup mild vegetable oil

Combine garlic, lime juice, mustard, mint leaves, sugar, salt, and pepper to taste in a small bowl.

With a whisk, add oil, a few drops at a time, beating vigorously until emulsified. Taste for seasonings and adjust.

AFTERTHOUGHT: Feel free to use a food processor to speed things up.

CHAPON

Rubbing the wooden salad bowl with a garlic clove may impart a whiff to a salad, but it will eventually ruin the bowl, making it smell rancid and feel gummy. Try, instead, the French method of using garlic discreetly—a chapon.

Rub a dry piece of bread with a peeled, cut clove of garlic. Toss lightly with the greens and dressing. Contrary to the directions usually given, only the cowardly will discard the chapon after tossing the salad. Eat it yourself, or share it with you best friend—and good health to you both.

SAUCES

ROUILLE

About 1 cup

A voluptuous sauce of garlic and pimientos. Serve it with fish soup, bouillabaisse, boiled potatoes, pasta, and, of course, broiled fish or chicken. Believe it or not, this stuff is great on crackers.

3 egg yolks	*2–3 tablespoons lemon juice*
4 garlic cloves, peeled	*3 canned red pimientos*
2 slices toasted bread, broken up	*Pinch of cayenne (or to taste)*
½ teaspoon salt	*1 cup olive oil*

Combine egg yolks, garlic, bread, salt, lemon juice, pimientos, and cayenne in a blender or food processor. Blend 1 minute.

While blender is running, add 1/2 cup olive oil, drop by drop, until incorporated, then add remaining 1/2 cup in a *very* thin stream, until it has reached the consistency of mayonnaise. Use immediately or cover and store in refrigerator up to two days.

AFTERTHOUGHT: A few leaves of basil or oregano, pounded in a mortar, may be added to the finished sauce. Do not put the herbs in the blender or food processor.

SALSA VERDE

1 2/3 cups

Delicious served with steamed broccoli, green beans, cauliflower, or asparagus.

1 cup firmly packed watercress leaves	*1 large garlic clove*
1 cup firmly packed parsley leaves, stems removed	*1 small onion, coarsely chopped*
	1 large hard-boiled egg
	2 anchovy fillets, rinsed

1 tablespoon capers, drained
⅓ cup red wine vinegar
1 cup light olive oil

Salt
Freshly ground pepper

Purée all ingredients except olive oil, salt, and pepper in a food processor.

With the motor running, add the oil in a thin stream to emulsify. Add salt and pepper to taste and blend briefly.

LEMON AND GARLIC VINAIGRETTE

About 1 1/2 cups

For broiled fish.

2 lemons
⅓ cup red wine vinegar
Salt to taste
⅔ cup olive oil
Freshly ground black pepper

¼ cup chopped fresh parsley
¼ cup chopped fresh tarragon or
   basil
2 garlic cloves, minced fine

Peel lemons carefully, removing all white membrane, and slice thin.

Place vinegar and salt in a bowl and stir to dissolve salt.

Add lemon slices and remaining ingredients; combine thoroughly. When the fish comes hot from the broiler, spoon the sauce over it and serve immediately.

PESTO

About 2 cups

Pesto is not just for pasta. Try it with steamed or poached fish, steamed broccoli, in hot rice, or with mayonnaise as a dipping sauce for crudités.

2 cups fresh basil leaves, washed
 and dried
3–4 garlic cloves, chopped
1 cup walnut meats or pine
 nuts
1 cup best olive oil

1 cup freshly grated Parmesan
 cheese
or
½ cup Parmesan, ½ cup
 Romano
Salt
Freshly ground black pepper

Combine basil, garlic, and nuts in a blender or food processor.

Add olive oil in a steady stream while motor continues running.

Add cheese, a bit of salt, and a grinding or two of pepper, and blend briefly. Transfer to a covered container and keep refrigerated until ready to use.

AÏOLI
(Garlic Mayonnaise)

Aïoli intoxicates gently, fills the body with
warmth, and the soul with enthusiasm. In its
essence it concentrates the strength, the gaiety
of the Provençal sunshine.
—Mistral

This sauce has been called "the butter of the sun," "the soul of the South," and "the butter of Provence,"—and it is as exhilarating as it sounds.

Beloved in Provence, aïoli is a legendary dish of banquets and the star of village fêtes. In the summer every village celebrates its saint's day; the main event is a great feast—the huge *aïoli monstre.* Long tables are set up in the town square, and everyone gathers to enjoy and share a nearly endless variety of meat, fish, snails, cod, chicken, eggs, and raw and cooked vegetables—all served with great bowls of aïoli. Robust red wine and iced water accompany this elaborate feast, and extended naps follow.

There are two hotly debated methods of making aïoli, but whichever one you choose, the freshest, crispest garlic is a must.

Just remember this: folklore tells us that drafts, germinating garlic cloves, and disloyal wives are supposed to cause the aïoli to curdle.

MORTAR AND PESTLE METHOD: THE CLASSIC

1 1/2 cups

Place 8 to 10 peeled, mashed garlic cloves, 2 room-temperature egg yolks, and salt to taste in a mortar. Pound with the pestle until the ingredients have turned into a paste. Then, while stirring constantly with the pestle, slowly begin pouring 1 1/2 cups oil (half peanut and half olive) in a steady, thin stream. Keep stirring constantly until a thick, shiny, firm sauce is obtained. Add the juice of 1 lemon and pepper to taste, and stir for 1 minute longer. Refrigerate until ready to use.

FOOD PROCESSOR METHOD: IRREVERENT AND MINE (SAME INGREDIENTS)

Purée garlic in a food processor. Whisk the egg yolks until smooth and add to the garlic. Add salt, pepper, and lemon juice, and blend to a smooth paste. With the machine still running, pour the oil in a very thin, steady stream into the garlic mixture. Continue blending until a thick, shiny, firm sauce is obtained. Transfer to a storage container and refrigerate until serving time.

AFTERTHOUGHTS: Serve aïoli with raw or lightly cooked vegetables, hard-boiled eggs, fish such as cod or tuna, grilled beef, or compose your own *aïoli monstre.*

You may also make a lighter version as follows: In a mortar combine salt and garlic and a warm boiled, peeled potato, and beat together until smooth. Add as much oil as you need to make a smooth, firm mixture. Now add the lemon juice and black pepper, blending again. This is a wonderful addition to vegetable soups, as well as part of a vegetable platter.

Aïoli is delicious with the addition of 1 teaspoon Dijon mustard. In fact, the *aïoli monstre* mixture contains it. Add it along with the egg yolks.

Another spiffy variation is to add 1 teaspoon freshly grated orange peel and 3 teaspoons fresh orange juice. A sunny sauce for soups with shellfish.

DELICATE GARLIC SAUCE

1 1/2 cups

Serve with fish, shellfish, pot-au-feu, or angel hair pasta, just for starters.

3 large garlic cloves,
  triple-blanched (page 6) and
  peeled
¾ cup fish broth
¾ cup dry white wine

3 shallots, minced
2 cups heavy cream
1 teaspoon lime juice
Salt to taste
1 tablespoon snipped chives

Press garlic through a strainer to purée. Reserve.

Bring broth, wine, and shallots to a boil in a heavy saucepan, and continue cooking at high heat approximately 20 minutes, until liquid is reduced to 2 tablespoons.

Add cream and simmer until reduced to 1 1/2 cups, about 15 minutes. Blend in puréed garlic and lime juice, and season to taste with salt. Garnish with chives.

BAGNA CAUDA

About 1 cup

Hot and jazzy. It won't be any problem to get them to eat their green vegetables with this sauce to dunk in.

½ cup olive oil
8 tablespoons butter

2 teaspoons finely minced garlic
10–12 anchovy fillets, drained

Melt the butter with the oil over low heat. Stir in the garlic and sauté slowly until garlic softens and begins to purée. Do not let it brown. The entire cooking time should be 5 to 6 minutes.

Add anchovy fillets and crush with a wooden spoon as you incorporate them into the sauce.

Keep warm over a low burner or in a chafing dish. Serve with a selection of raw and/or lightly parboiled vegetables and crusty bread.

BAGNA ROTOU

About 3/4 cup

Serve this wonderful sauce with raw or cooked warm or cold vegetables, cold sliced meats, or shellfish.

2 tablespoons red wine vinegar	*2 large garlic cloves, finely*
Salt to taste	*minced*
6 tablespoons good olive oil	*1 tablespoon chopped fresh basil*
Freshly ground black pepper	*¼ cup chopped fresh parsley*
1 small onion, minced fine	*4 anchovy fillets, drained*
	1 tablespoon capers (optional)

Mix vinegar and salt in a bowl. Whisk in oil until emulsified. Add remaining ingredients and blend well. Adjust seasonings.

AFTERTHOUGHT: Improves with age and keeps well (if nobody finds it).

GARLIC CONSERVE

About 1 1/2 cups

The next time you roast a leg or rack of lamb—or better yet, throw a butterflied, marinated leg of lamb on the grill—why don't you run up a little batch of this garlic conserve? It's lusty and unusual, and fabulous with lamb in any form.

1 pound garlic cloves, coarsely	*½ cup water or white wine*
chopped	*¾ cup sugar*
¾ cup sherry wine vinegar	

Combine all the ingredients in a heavy saucepan. Bring to a boil over high heat, stirring constantly.

Reduce the heat to very low and simmer, stirring occasionally, until the garlic is very soft, and the mixture is light, golden, and slightly syrupy, 20 to 25 minutes.

Scrape the conserve into a small bowl and allow it to cool. (It keeps well, covered, in the refrigerator for a week.) Serve at room temperature.

ESCARGOT BUTTER

About 1 cup

So called because it is the classic flavored butter served on snails. It's not too shabby on clams, either!

½ pound butter, softened to room temperature
3–4 garlic cloves, finely minced

¼ cup finely chopped parsley
2 tablespoons finely minced shallots

Beat all the ingredients together until well blended. Chill in the mixing bowl or form into a roll as explained for Garlic Butter (recipe follows).

GARLIC BUTTER

1/2 cup

Indispensable!

8 tablespoons butter, at room temperature
2–3 garlic cloves, finely minced (or more to taste)

Fresh parsley, finely minced
Lemon juice (optional)

Beat softened butter and garlic together in a small bowl. (This recipe works very well in a food processor or blender, especially if you are making larger amounts.)

Add parsley, lemon juice, and any other herbs or seasonings you may like—there is no end to the flavored butters you can create. Blend ingredients thoroughly. Serve immediately or chill for later use.

AFTERTHOUGHTS: You may re-form the butter into a roll as follows: With a rubber spatula, form the butter into a tube shape on a sheet of wax paper that has been placed on a slightly longer sheet of aluminum foil. Roll up the butter and twist the foil ends in opposite directions to hold the roll's shape. Chill until firm; then cut in slices to serve on hot fish, meats, or steamed vegetables. This butter is wonderful for grilled sandwiches, too.

VARIATIONS

For shallot butter, omit garlic and add more shallots.

Chive butter? Use lots or add some scallions.

For scallion butter, use tops and bulbs.

GARLIC ICE CREAM

About 2 cups

From the legendary *Alice B. Toklas Cookbook,* here is a unique recipe. It's really her sauce for avocados, with an amusing name.

4 small tomatoes, peeled, seeded, and chopped to a pulp
1 tablespoon Worcestershire sauce
1 teaspoon Tabasco sauce
½ teaspoon salt

4 cloves garlic, double-blanched and peeled (page 6)
1 cup mayonnaise
Several drops liquid smoke
1 teaspoon onion juice

Beat the ingredients until they are well mixed. Freeze, covered. Do not stir while freezing.

Serve in halved avocados.

BREADS

BRUSCHETTA
Italian-style Garlic Toast

This is surely one of the glories of Italian country food.

1 loaf crusty Italian or French   *Coarse salt*
  bread, sliced   *Garlic cloves, peeled*
Your finest olive oil

Toast bread slices over a grill, a charcoal fire, or, if all else fails, in a very hot oven (425–450°F) until lightly browned. Remove from heat and brush lavishly with a fine, fruity olive oil. Serve warm with a bowl of peeled garlic cloves and one of coarse salt. Have your guests simply rub their bread with one of the cloves and sprinkle with salt. Pass a platter of rich, ripe tomato slices and leaves of fresh basil and stand back!

GARLIC PITA TOASTS

48 triangles

I keep a jar of these crispy toasts on hand at all times, and I blush to tell you that I adore them with a spoonful of golden caviar and a glass of bubbly—a great restorative in this imperfect world.

4 tablespoons butter   *1 small garlic clove, minced*
⅓ cup olive oil   *6 pita loaves*
1 teaspoon poppy seeds   *Salt to taste*

Preheat oven to 300°F.

    Melt the butter and oil together in a small saucepan. Add poppy seeds and garlic and keep warm.

    Cut the pita loaves into quarters and separate each one into two triangles. Brush the rough side of each triangle lightly with the butter mixture. Sprinkle with salt if you like it.

Arrange the triangles, buttered side up, on a cookie sheet. Bake them in the preheated oven for 1 hour, or until they are very crisp and lightly golden. Serve warm or cool. After cooling they may be stored in a tightly closed container.

AFTERTHOUGHT: I often like to sprinkle mine with grated Parmesan or Romano before baking.

GARLIC BREAD

For one large loaf

I had this bread on my honeymoon. We ate it with great bowls of rattling good cioppino.

8 tablespoons butter, softened
½ cup fresh olive oil
½ cup freshly grated Parmesan or Romano cheese, the best you can buy
1 teaspoon poppy seeds
1 teaspoon aniseed

1 teaspoon caraway seeds
2–3 garlic cloves, very finely minced
1 teaspoon paprika
⅓ cup minced fresh parsley
1 loaf French bread

Preheat oven to 400°F.

Cream the butter, oil, and cheese together.

Add the remaining ingredients except bread and blend well.

Now for the fun: Take a long loaf of French bread, sweet or sourdough; it doesn't matter. Slice it on the diagonal almost through, managing to leave the slices attached at the bottom. Spread one side of each slice generously with the mixture. Push the loaf back into its shape and then slather the top and sides.

Wrap the loaf in foil and place it in the preheated oven for 15 to 20 minutes. Serve it forth and accept the applause with modesty.

AFTERTHOUGHT: This luscious spread also works well on slices of bread broiled just until they sizzle and the edges begin to brown.

JOE SILLANO'S
GARLIC BREAD FOR A CROWD

Serves 100

Here is a recipe from the world-famous Gilroy garlic festival. If the wind's blowing in the right direction, you can probably smell it in Minnesota. The bread is supposed to serve 100, if they're not too hungry.

2 pounds butter	*Salt*
2 pounds margarine	*Freshly ground black pepper*
3 cups corn oil	*¼ teaspoon crushed dried red*
1 cup water	*chilies (optional)*
4–5 heads garlic	*15–20 loaves French bread*
4 bay leaves	*Chopped fresh parsley*
½ cup dried rosemary	

Combine butter, margarine, oil, and water in a large shallow pan. Place on grill over hot coals or over low heat. Separate, peel, and crush garlic cloves. Add to butter mixture. Place bay leaves and rosemary in a cheesecloth bag and add to butter mixture. Add salt and pepper to taste and crushed chilies. Cook over low heat about 40 minutes, until garlic is nearly dissolved, stirring occasionally.

Cut bread in half lengthwise and toast on grill, turning once. When ready to serve, remove cheesecloth bag and stir in chopped parsley to taste.

Dip cut sides of bread into butter mixture, remove to cutting board, and slice in large chunks. Serve at once.

MUFFALETTA

Serves six

An extraordinary Italian sandwich.

3 large garlic cloves, crushed
1 cup pimiento-stuffed olives,
  chopped
1 cup pitted black olives, chopped
½ cup roasted sweet peppers, cut
  into large pieces (either
  homemade or Progresso)
1 cup best olive oil
4 tablespoons chopped parsley

2 tablespoons red wine vinegar
  (or more to taste)
Freshly ground black pepper to
  taste
1 large Italian or French loaf
⅓ pound Italian salami, sliced
½ pound provolone cheese, sliced
½ pound Havarti cheese, sliced
⅓ pound prosciutto

The day before you plan to serve muffaletta, prepare the salad by combining the garlic, olives, peppers, olive oil, parsley, vinegar, and pepper. Cover and let stand overnight.

To assemble sandwich, slice bread in half horizontally. Remove some of the center of the loaf to make room for the filling (save and use for bread crumbs or bird food). Drizzle olive oil from the salad on both halves—heavily.

On bottom half of loaf lay salami, provolone, Havarti, olive salad, and prosciutto. Top with second half and slice into wedges if round loaf, or in rounds if long.

GARLIC CROUTONS I

1 cup

For salads, light soups, and stuffings.

2 tablespoons clarified butter
2 tablespoons light olive oil
2 garlic cloves, minced

1 cup diced bread, crusts
  trimmed
Salt

Combine butter and olive oil in an 8-inch frying pan and heat over a medium flame for a minute or so. Add bread cubes and garlic, and toss continually until the cubes are golden brown, about 1 minute. Remove croutons from pan and drain on paper towels. Salt them lightly and they are ready to use.

GARLIC CROUTONS II

About 4 cups

These are a sensation in hearty soups and green salads.

12 slices French bread, about 1 inch thick, crusts removed
2 cups peanut oil

3–4 large garlic cloves, halved lengthwise

Cut the bread slices into triangles. Place the peanut oil in a heavy saucepan and heat until a cube of bread will brown in 30 seconds. Fry the triangles, six or eight at a time. As they brown, remove them from the oil, and drain on paper towels.

Rub each triangle with a cut clove of garlic. Use at once or stash them in a zip-lock bag, making certain that the zip is locked.

CROÛTES

Indispensable for soups and salads.

1-inch slices of French bread
Olive oil

Garlic cloves, halved lengthwise

Preheat oven to 325°F.

Place bread slices on a baking sheet and brush generously with olive oil. Rub bread lightly with the cut garlic.

Bake approximately 45 minutes, or until light golden in color and crisp, turning once during baking.

2 The Incomparable Onion

> Banish it from the kitchen and the pleasure of eating flies with it. Its presence lends color and enchantment to the most modest dish; its absence reduces the rarest delicacy to hopeless insipidity, and the diner to despair.
> —Elizabeth Robbins Pennell

While the flowering lilies of the field, so the Bible tells us, are famous for neither spinning nor weaving, their edible onion cousins, in all their forms and colors, have nourished and sustained us since the first person pulled one from the earth and ate it with relish along with his broiled dinosaur. From that time on, this ancient, versatile family member has proliferated, wild and cultivated, all over this beautiful green earth.

The ubiquitous onion has a long, distinguished history and, like garlic, has been endowed with healing properties and mystical significance. For the ancient Egyptians, the onion's nine encircling layers represented eternity. Two thousand years ago, Egyptian princes were reputed to have spent ninety tons of gold buying them just to keep the workmen laboring on the pyramids in good health and spirits. That's a *lot* of gold and a *whole lot* of onions—I mean, they BELIEVED!

A vegetable for all seasons, the noble, indispensable onion is always in abundant supply; it's cheap and filled with B vitamins, vitamin C, iron, calcium, potassium, and protein, i.e. it's *good* for you. In addition, onions look great just waiting around the kitchen.

Consider the onions: they come in pleasing shapes, many sizes, and several colors—ivory, red, golden brown, and green. They are full of surprising flavors: pungent, sweet, hot, spicy, and mellow. Their textures are crisp, pearly, and full of juice when raw; a long, slow simmering and they become velvety and smooth. Sautéed gently, their natural sugar gives them a beautiful, rich brown color, and that's what we're after, heh?

Onions may be pickled, creamed, roasted, stuffed, puréed, French fried, sautéed, stir-fried, scalloped, and grilled. What is soup without onions? Or how about onion marmalade, relish, chutney, tart, custard, and pudding? Then there's onion sorbet, onion bread, pizza, muffins, biscuits, pancakes, dumplings, salads, sauces, snacks, and garnishes—or simply raw. How's that for versatile?

The spirited onion and all its aromatic relations are, quite simply, fundamental to good cooking, and the genial companion of savory dishes. In solo numbers of their own, they star with brio. Altogether, the lilies of the kitchen are an elegant bunch and richly deserve the celebrations of them that we share, for what would we do without them? If they didn't exist, it would be necessary to invent them—and that's the truth.

> There is in every cook's opinion
> No savory dish without an onion.
> —Dean Swift

Technique

> I must understand onions. If you cook them a little while, you get a light sugar. If you cook them a little longer, you get too much sugar. When I know how to cook onions, then I will be good.

These pertinent words are from Marc Meneau, chef of the three-star restaurant, Espérance, in Vézelay, France. I lunched in that beautiful place last summer and, clearly, he knows his onions.

Now I'm going to tell you how I feel about onions. There are several varieties on the market at all times, not counting the exotic new varieties like the Vidalias from Georgia, the sweet, sturdy Walla-Wallas from Washington state, or the glorious onions from Maui. The standard family members include:

Spanish Onions: Not from Spain at all, these are large, globe-shaped, and usually golden brown. Mild and sweet, and available fall and winter.

Globe Onions: The most common onions. Usually available with yellow skins, but sometimes white or red. All-purpose.

Red Italian Onions: The mildest of all. Available in spring and summer.

Granos: Pungent and globe-shaped, these yellow onions can be found up to 5 inches in diameter.

Bermuda Onions: These ivory-colored, flattish onions really do come from Bermuda. Available April to June, they are sweet and crisp.

Pearl Onions: Also called white onions; sometimes Spanish. They are small, firm, and sweet. Baby pearls are the tiniest of the white crop.

Now, they are all good; some are better than others; some are a great deal more expensive—but they're all good. Personally, I have never found that much difference in flavor between the golden, ivory, silver, or brown ones. True, the red ones are best eaten raw, but that's about it.

It's important to use a little horse sense when you choose onions. Be sure that the skins are shiny and dry. They should have absolutely *no* smell whatever. If they do, they are probably bruised somewhere under the skin and are on their way out. Don't buy onions that are beginning to sprout unless you just want to watch them turn into a green bouquet. Young onions are sweeter than old ones, but alas, the age of onions is harder to determine than the age of some movie queens.

The way you handle an onion is the most important thing, not its name, size, age, color, price, or place of origin.

When you get them home, having chosen them in several sizes (for different purposes, silly), keep them in a cool, airy place (not in the refrigerator). A basket will do. See that they are kept dry, and that's the care of onions.

Now for the matter of slicing, chopping, etc. Admittedly, it can be a teary business. You can fiddle around with the old wives' tales and cut them holding a match or crust of bread in your teeth, do it under water, and so forth; or you can take this old wife's advice and get yourself a fine, sharp, well-balanced knife, learn to use it effectively and with some speed, and be done with it.

The only other things I can think of to prevent a few tears is to chop your onions wearing a diver's helmet or a scuba diving mask, but that seems a little excessive. I have heard chilling them an hour or so works. Personally, I wear my reading glasses, and that may help.

By the way, if by chance you find that you have half an onion left over, be brave and throw it out. Something very unpleasant happens to cut onions that are not used promptly; probably the sulfur content, so don't bother to wrap it up and save it for another day. Out with it!

If you just want a little onion juice, scrape a cut half with a sharp knife.

One pound of onions equals 4 cups sliced or chopped, 2 cups cooked, and 3 to 4 servings.

One last thing—do cook onions *slowly* (except, of course, for deep frying). Gentle cooking renders them sweet and mellow. If you burn them, toss them out and start again.

Now, how about some Sage and Onion Pudding (page 123) for dinner?

FIRST COURSES

DAUSSADES

Serves six

Once upon a time, one rainy summer day in France, hungry, damp, lost, and tired in a hill town overlooking the stormy Mediterranean, I found a tiny auberge. Just like in the books, the patron welcomed me warmly and led me to a tiny table beside the fire. Before I could even slip out of my damp shoes he reappeared with a glass of red wine, a basket of crisp rolls, and a heavenly dish that he called *daussades*. Whatever you call it, it is bliss. This recipe is as close as I can come to the delicious dish that warmed and restored me on that stormy day.

The long, slow cooking of the onions produces a thick, velvety sauce, sweet and a little tart. (The minced ham doesn't hurt either.)

4 *tablespoons butter*	1¼ *cups full-bodied red wine*
3 *pounds medium-size red*	*such as Zinfandel or Petit*
onions, halved lengthwise and	*Sirah*
thinly sliced	*Salt*
1 *tablespoon balsamic vinegar*	*Freshly ground black pepper*
	Sherry wine vinegar
	¼ *cup minced baked ham*

In a 4-quart enameled or stainless steel saucepan, melt the butter over low heat. Add onions, swirl them around, cover, and sweat them for 45 minutes, stirring occasionally.

Uncover and increase the heat to medium-high. Cook, stirring frequently, until the onions are glazed and golden, about 15 minutes. Add the balsamic vinegar and boil down for 2–3 minutes to glaze further.

Reduce heat to low, add the wine, and cook, stirring often, until the onions are soft and a beautiful deep brown, 1 1/2 to 2 hours.

Season with salt, a grinding or two of black pepper, and a tablespoon or so of sherry wine vinegar. Stir in the ham. Serve hot, at room temperature, or warm.

AFTERTHOUGHTS: Daussades is wonderful with crusty bread, on toast and served with drinks, with grilled chicken, or liver, or steak, or, or, or . . .

You may also like to try it with sweet Spanish onions.

This will keep, refrigerated, for 2 or 3 days, so don't wait for a rainy day—make it sometime when you have a few hours, then get it out and warm it up when you need it. It will be a star in your culinary crown; that's a promise.

VIDALIA ONION TARTS

Serves six

What we have here is a summit meeting of the trendy. Nevertheless, it's delicious. The sweet Vidalias are complemented perfectly by the fresh, tart chèvre, and served on thin, buttery crusts. It's not a dish to be trifled with.

1 package frozen puff pastry, defrosted
2 tablespoons butter
2 medium Vidalia onions, chopped (or Mauis or Walla-Wallas)
1 small sweet red pepper, cored, seeded, and diced
2 tablespoons currants
2 tablespoons lemon juice

1 teaspoon mild honey
½ teaspoon grated fresh ginger
½ teaspoon turmeric
Salt
Freshly ground black pepper
3 tablespoons dry vermouth
6 generous tablespoons chèvre (Montrachet or Bucheron would be nice)
Minced chives

Cut puff pastry into six 4-inch rounds and bake according to package directions.

Melt butter in a heavy skillet and sauté onions and red pepper until tender. Add currants, lemon juice, honey, ginger, turmeric, salt, pepper, and vermouth and simmer until thickened. Watch carefully so mixture does not burn.

Mound onion mixture on finished puff pastry rounds. Crumble one tablespoon of chèvre onto each tart and serve spangled with minced chives.

ONION CHEESE EMPANADITAS

About 30

Serve these spicy little turnovers with drinks.

1 cup chopped onion
4 tablespoons butter
1 hard-boiled egg, diced
2 pimientos, diced
1 tablespoon minced pickled
jalapeño, or 2 tablespoons
green chili sauce
1 cup shredded sharp Cheddar
cheese
2 heaping tablespoons
mayonnaise

Salt
Freshly ground black pepper
Pastry for a 2-crust 9-inch pie,
homemade, or from 1 package
Betty Crocker's pie crust mix
(no kidding; it's very good)
1 egg yolk whisked with 2
tablespoons water

Sauté the onions in the butter until tender. Cool slightly. In a bowl, combine egg, pimiento, jalapeño, cheese, mayonnaise, and onions, and mix well. Season with salt and pepper to taste.

Preheat oven to 400°F.

Roll pastry out on a lightly floured board about 1/16 inch thick (that's thin). Cut pastry into 3-inch rounds. Place a teaspoon of filling in the center of each circle. With your fingers, lightly coat the edges with a little of the egg glaze. Fold in half and seal with tines of a fork.

Bake for 15 to 20 minutes. Serve hot. (I've eaten them cold, and they're also very good.)

AFTERTHOUGHTS: This mixture works fine spread on rounds of Melba toast and broiled.

It wouldn't be bad mixed into a freshly baked potato, either.

It makes a great open-face sandwich, cold or broiled.

If you have cilantro available, chop a few leaves and add to the onion mixture.

Add chopped black olives to the mixture, too. Or green ones. Delicious!

ESCABECHE
(Fillets of Fish Marinated
in Citrus Vinaigrette)

Serves six

On the day my friend Val Edwards returned from an adventurous cruise in the West Indies (where he researched the island cuisine and several of the local maidens), he rolled up his sleeves, tore into the kitchen, and prepared this lively dish to the delight of two Swedish newspapermen and the other visiting firemen who happened along the next day.

Along with the fish he fixed a mountain of freshly shucked sweet corn, brushed with melted butter and roasted over charcoal until it was golden and browned here and there. We also destroyed a mess of fine barbecued ribs. Ripe sweet melons finished off this eye-popping feast. The Swedes will never be the same.

1 orange
Flour
6 fillets of mackerel, red snapper, or sea bass, about 4 ounces each
¾ cup olive oil
1 red onion, sliced into thin rings
1 green pepper, cored, seeded, and sliced into thin rings

½ cup fresh orange juice
¼ cup fresh lime juice
2 garlic cloves, minced
1 jalapeño pepper, raw or pickled, seeded and chopped
Salt
Freshly ground black pepper

Cut the peel off the orange, leaving the pith. Slice into julienne and blanch in boiling water for 1 minute. Drain, pat dry, and place in a plastic bag. Store in refrigerator until needed.

Lightly flour the fish fillets. Heat 1/4 cup of the oil until hot, but not smoking. Sauté the fish for 2 minutes on each side. Remove pan from heat and carefully transfer the fillets to a ceramic or glass dish just large enough to hold them in a single layer. Top with the onion and pepper rings.

Add remaining olive oil to the skillet and heat until warm. Add orange and lime juice, garlic, and chopped chili. Bring the marinade to a boil, swirling the skillet. Taste for seasonings, add salt and pepper as needed, and pour over the fish. Allow the marinade to cool; cover and chill overnight.

To serve, transfer half the peppers and onions to a serving plate. Place the fillets on top of the vegetables, top with remaining onions and peppers, and garnish with the julienned orange rind.

SOUPS

A SIMPLE STOCK

About 2 quarts

The foundation of good soup.

2–3 *pounds sawed beef or veal bones*
2 *large carrots, scrubbed and cut into chunks*
3 *large onions, unpeeled and quartered*

Large herb bouquet (3 unpeeled garlic cloves, 8 sprigs parsley, 1 large bay leaf, 1 teaspoon dried thyme, 4 whole cloves, a few peppercorns, all tied in cheesecloth)
Salt to taste

Preheat oven to 450°F.

Spread the bones, carrots, and onions in a roomy roasting pan and roast them for about 40 minutes. Baste now and then with the accumulated fat in the pan, turning them once or twice. When they are a fine, rich brown, transfer them with a slotted spoon to a soup pot.

Discard the fat and deglaze the pan: pour a cup or so of water into the pan and set it over direct heat. Scrape all the brown roasting bits and juices into the water. Pour this into the soup kettle, add enough water to cover all the ingredients, and bring to a boil. Add the herb bouquet, cover partially, and simmer for 4 to 5 hours. Taste for salt and add as necessary. Cool.

Strain into a large bowl and discard bones, vegetables, and herb bouquet. Chill thoroughly and then peel off the fat that has risen to the surface. Your stock is ready.

AFTERTHOUGHT: You may use the stock as is, or reduce it further, until it becomes almost syrupy, being careful toward the end—it burns easily. Reduced to this stage, it will keep for months in the fridge, ready at all times to enrich a stew, another soup, or make terrific gravy. It may also be frozen in an ice cube tray, and there you have handy little cubes of fine meat glaze, ready to use.

"THE" ONION SOUP

Serves six

Onion soup, delicate and creamy. Onion soup with red wine. Rich brown onion soup laden with melting Gruyère. Onion soup with garlicky croutons—take your choice; they are all superb.

Onion soup is a dish of quintessential simplicity, requiring only a few ingredients and your care and attention in the preparation. But note: the line between a bland, nothing soup and a mellow, satisfying, world-class one is very thin. Here is a killer of the second variety.

3 tablespoons butter
1 tablespoon olive oil
5–6 large onions (about 1½ pounds), thinly sliced
½ teaspoon sugar
1 teaspoon salt
1 large garlic clove, thinly sliced
2 tablespoons flour
2 quarts hot beef stock (see A Simple Stock, page 79, or, in a pinch, canned beef broth)
2 cups very drinkable dry red wine

Dash of red wine vinegar
Pinch of thyme
Few grindings of black pepper
Bay leaf
1 loaf firm French bread, made into 1-inch croûtes (see page 68)
1 pound Gruyère, or a good, nutty Switzerland Swiss cheese, diced small
Freshly grated Parmesan cheese
Melted butter

Melt the butter and olive oil together in a heavy, 4-quart soup pot. Add the onions, cover, and cook over low heat for 15 to 20 minutes, stirring occasionally.

Raise the heat to moderate, uncover pan, and add sugar and salt. Cook 20 to 30 minutes longer, stirring frequently, until the onions have turned a rich, mahogany brown.

Reduce heat to low, add the garlic, and cook 1 minute. Blend in the flour and cook, stirring constantly, for 2 to 3 minutes. Remove the pan from the heat and blend in 1 cup of hot stock, making sure the flour is completely dissolved. Stir in the remaining stock, the wine, vinegar, thyme, and pepper, and bring to a boil. Lower heat and simmer slowly, cover slightly ajar, for 30 minutes. Add bay leaf the last 15 minutes, discarding it at the end of cooking time. Taste for seasonings and adjust as needed.

NOTE: The soup can be prepared several days in advance (in fact, it improves with age), but if you are planning to serve it gratinée, have your guests clamoring at the table as you remove it from the broiler, or the crust will sink like a leaky barge. Therefore:

Preheat broiler.

Smear a bit of butter in the bottom of individual earthenware (or other heatproof) bowls, and place them on a cookie sheet. Place a croûte on the bottom of each bowl and sprinkle generously with Gruyère. Repeat this procedure in each bowl. Ladle in the simmering soup. Float another croûte on top of each serving, sprinkle on more Gruyère and a drift of Parmesan. Drizzle with a bit of melted butter, and whisk the bowls under the preheated broiler for a few minutes. Watch carefully. When the cheese is crusty and the soup bubbling, serve immediately.

AFTERTHOUGHTS: Serve the soup with Bruschetta or Garlic Croutons (pages 64 and 67).

Try Bruschetta smeared with a little Dijon mustard and topped with Brie in place of the Gruyère croûtes.

If you're feeling like a high roller, add a dash of Cognac to each serving when you ladle on the soup.

If you're concerned about your weight, serve the soup unadorned except for a sprinkling of fresh minced parsley. Pass thin Bruschetta or lightly toasted French bread and a small bowl of grated Parmesan at the table.

You may also wish to serve the soup from a tureen. Preheat oven to 425°F, and bake for about 30 minutes, or until brown and crusty.

And do try the redoubtable Julia Child's version: a couple of egg yolks beaten with 4 or 5 tablespoons of port or Madeira, poured under the edge of the crust, and gently stirred just before serving. (Divide this amount among bowls if serving them individually.)

BLACK BEAN SOUP

Serves six to eight

From Brazil comes this carnival in a bowl. Garnished with *brio*, it's hot stuff, lusty, and satisfying.

2 cups dried black beans, washed
1 ham hock
4 garlic cloves, unpeeled and
    mashed
1 large onion, unpeeled and
    quartered
2 carrots, thickly sliced
1 teaspoon cumin seeds
1 teaspoon dried red pepper
    flakes

2 quarts water
½ cup good rum

GARNISH
Chicharrones (see Afterthoughts)
Fresh herbs
Pickled jalapeños
Cilantro leaves
Chopped red onions
Vinegar and oil

Combine all soup ingredients except rum in a large, heavy kettle. Bring to a boil, reduce heat, and simmer until beans are soft, approximately 2 hours.

When beans are tender, remove from heat and allow to cool thoroughly. Remove garlic, onion, and carrots and discard. Remove meat from ham hock, chop coarsely, and set aside.

Remove a little over half the beans from the stock with a slotted spoon. Purée them in a blender or food processor and set aside.

Skim fat from stock and discard. Combine puréed beans with stock, adding more liquid if necessary. Return ham to soup. Taste for seasonings and adjust as needed. Add rum and heat soup slowly before serving.

Serve soup in individual heated soup bowls accompanied by crumbled chicharrones, chopped fresh herbs (oregano, basil, rosemary, parsley, chives, etc.), chopped pickled jalapeños, cilantro, chopped red onions, and cruets of vinegar and oil. Let your guests help themselves.

AFTERTHOUGHTS: For an interesting variation, try serving the soup with bowls of chopped pickled Maui onions (sweet or hot), Mexican cream, and salsa verde. Mexican cream is the Latino counterpart of crème fraîche, and can be used in the same way. I hope you have a Mexican market nearby.

Garlic Pita Toasts (page 64) would be a nice accompaniment.

Chicharrones, by the way, are crisp fried pork rinds (I know this sounds terrible but, trust me, they are great crumbled into this soup). They are to be found in Mexican markets.

CARROT AND ORANGE SOUP

Serves six

Beneath the surface of this smiling soup, a touch of Tabasco renders it anything but bland. Light and refreshing, yes. Bland, no.

12 large carrots, peeled and chopped
3 onions, chopped
1 quart chicken broth
4 tablespoons butter
1 cup fresh orange juice
Salt
Freshly ground black pepper

2–3 tablespoons Outerbridge Sauce (see Afterthought) or a few drops of Tabasco (or to taste)
Sour cream
Chopped chives
Grated orange peel

Simmer the carrots and onions in the broth in a large covered saucepan until very soft, about 30 minutes.

Strain the solids and purée them in a food processor or blender. Return to broth.

Add the butter, orange juice, and seasonings, and simmer for 5 minutes. Taste for seasonings and adjust. Serve hot or cold, garnished with sour cream, chives, and grated orange peel.

AFTERTHOUGHT: Outerbridge Sauce can be found in specialty food shops—it's great in Bloody Marys, too!

GREEN SOUP WITH CHILIES AND FRESH HERBS

Serves six

This piquant, colorful soup may be served hot or cold.

2 large onions, chopped
2 pounds young zucchini and summer squash
1 bunch spinach, washed, drained, stems removed, and torn
3 cups water
2 cups chicken broth
½ bottle (7 ounces) green chili sauce

Salt
Freshly ground black pepper
Lemon juice to taste
Sour cream
Chives
Handful of fresh green herbs (cilantro, parsley, oregano, thyme, basil, mint—any or all)

Simmer onions, squash, and spinach in water and broth until soft.

Purée vegetables in a blender or food processor. Add chili sauce, salt, pepper, and lemon juice and blend once more. Reheat if serving hot.

Serve in individual soup bowls garnished with sour cream, chives, and a drift of fresh herbs.

CELESTIAL CRAB SOUP

Serves six

Golden and shimmering, to call this luxurious potion a soup is like calling an emerald a green stone.

3 tablespoons olive oil
1 large onion, finely minced
2 large garlic cloves, finely minced
¼ teaspoon saffron threads, crushed
4½ cups fish stock (your own or see Appendix, "Tips on Ingredients")
⅓ cup dry white wine
½ cup fresh orange juice
¼ cup fresh grapefruit juice
4 thin lemon slices
Few slender parings of orange peel (use a potato peeler)

¼ teaspoon freshly grated lemon peel
1 teaspoon bitter orange marmalade
1 tablespoon tomato paste
1 bay leaf
1 pound crabmeat, flaked
Salt
6 slices French bread, about ½ inch thick, toasted
Aïoli with orange (page 59)
3 thin orange slices, halved
Minced fresh parsley

Heat olive oil in a large saucepan over medium heat. Add onion and cook, stirring occasionally, until it becomes translucent, about 5 minutes. Add the garlic and saffron and cook 2 minutes longer.

Blend in the stock, wine, juices, lemon slices, peels, marmalade, tomato paste, and the bay leaf and bring to a boil. Reduce heat to low, cover, and simmer for 10 minutes. Discard bay leaf. Add the crabmeat and salt to taste and simmer, uncovered, for 5 minutes, or until crabmeat is heated thoroughly but still tender.

Ladle the soup into individual heated soup bowls. Float a toasted bread slice on each serving and top with a tablespoon or so of aïoli. Garnish with half an orange slice and a sprinkling of parsley.

ENTRÉES

ONION AND POTATO FRITATTA

Serves four

In a pinch, this dish will always bail you out.

3 medium brown onions   3 tablespoons chopped chives
3 medium russet potatoes   Salt
¼ cup best olive oil   Freshly ground black pepper
8 large eggs, beaten lightly   Chopped parsley and chives
3 tablespoons chopped parsley   Fruity olive oil

Preheat broiler.

Peel the onions and potatoes and grate them into a bowl. (A food processor's grating attachment makes this a snap.) Place the mixture in a clean kitchen towel and squeeze out excess moisture.

Heat olive oil in a 12-inch iron skillet. Add potatoes and onions, cover, and sauté them for 10 minutes over medium-low heat. Watch carefully, adjusting heat as necessary to prevent the onions from browning; stir now and then. When mixture is tender and slightly creamy, remove from heat and cool slightly.

Combine the eggs, parsley, chives, salt, and a few grindings of pepper.

Return skillet to low heat and pour egg mixture over onions and potatoes. Cook slowly until bottom half of fritatta has set. Place skillet under hot broiler to set top. When golden brown, and a knife inserted in the middle comes out clean, the fritatta is ready. Do not let it overcook. Serve immediately right from the skillet, garnished with chopped parsley and chives and a fine drizzle of olive oil.

AFTERTHOUGHT: You can also bake the fritatta in a preheated 450°F. oven for about 20 minutes. (Reduce oven temperature if eggs cook too quickly.)

MAUI ONION TART

Serves four

Good stuff, but it just makes me want to jump on a plane to Maui.

*1 cup grated sharp Cheddar
   cheese*
*½ pound bacon, cooked and
   crumbled*
2 large Maui onions, shredded
¼ cup chopped parsley

½ cup half-and-half
2 cups milk
½ cup biscuit mix
4 eggs
¼ teaspoon salt
½ cup grated Parmesan cheese

Preheat oven to 350°F.

Combine the Cheddar, bacon, onions, parsley, and half-and-half. Spread the filling in a well-buttered 10-inch quiche pan. A deep pie pan will do.

Place the milk, biscuit mix, eggs, salt, and Parmesan in a blender. Process at high speed for 1 minute. Pour over the onion mixture in the pan.

Bake in the preheated oven for 55 minutes, or until a knife inserted in the middle comes out clean. Allow the tart to cool for 5 minutes before serving.

AFTERTHOUGHT: You may substitute 8 ounces Portuguese sausage for the bacon. To do this, slit the casing and crumble the sausage into a skillet. Sauté until brown and the fat is released. Drain and proceed as above.

PISSALADIÈRE

Serves six

A Provençal onion tart, crisp and light, whose variations are end-less.

¼ cup olive oil, plus more for
  crust
3 pounds medium onions, finely
  minced
2 garlic cloves, crushed
1 teaspoon dried thyme, oregano,
  or marjoram
Salt
Freshly ground black pepper

Onion Crust (recipe follows)
Cornmeal
6 anchovy fillets, drained and
  halved lengthwise
Oil-cured black olives, pitted and
  slivered
Fresh marjoram and/or basil
  leaves, minced

Heat olive oil in a large skillet with a lid. Add the onions, garlic, herbs, salt, and pepper. Cover tightly and simmer very slowly over the barest heat for 1 hour. (Do not try to rush this process. Only slow simmering produces the sweetest flavor.)

When the onions have become a golden purée, remove them from the heat. Press the onions gently against one side of the pan with a slotted spoon, and draw off the liquid that remains. Reserve this juice for the crust. Taste the onions for seasonings and adjust as necessary. Set aside.

Prepare the crust.

Preheat oven to 375°F.

Oil an 8x13-inch baking pan. Sprinkle with cornmeal.

Roll out the dough on a floured board. With your hands, pat and stretch the dough along the bottom and sides of the pan until it rises about 3/4 inch up the sides. Lightly oil the dough with olive oil.

Spoon the onion purée into the crust. Arrange anchovy fillets in a lattice pattern, and decorate with slivers of olives. Drizzle lightly with a bit more olive oil.

Bake in the preheated oven for about 1 hour, or until the crust has pulled away from the sides of the pan and is golden and crisp. Remove from the oven and sprinkle with fresh minced herbs. Serve hot or at room temperature.

ONION CRUST

¼ teaspoon active dry yeast
¼ cup lukewarm water
1 tablespoon reserved onion cooking liquid (add olive oil to make 1 tablespoon if not enough)

1 teaspoon salt
1 cup unbleached flour
Olive oil

Dissolve the yeast in water and let stand 5 minutes in a warm spot.

Stir in the onion liquid and salt. Add the flour and combine well.

Knead for 20 minutes or so on a floured board until the dough is smooth and soft. Place the ball in an oiled bowl, turning it in the bowl once or twice to lightly coat it with oil. Cover with a damp tea towel and leave in a warm place to double in size, approximately 1 hour.

Punch the ball down. Oil your hands lightly with olive oil and knead for 5 minutes longer. Cover and let the dough rise again for 10 minutes.

Proceed with rolling and filling.

GREEN PEPPER AND ONION PIE

Serves six

Who says real men don't eat quiche? The men I cook for love this one—there's never a crumb left over—ever. Try it and see for yourself.

1 large green pepper, seeds and stem removed, sliced in julienne
1 medium onion, sliced thin, separated into rings
3 tablespoons olive oil
Salt
Freshly ground black pepper

1 deep-dish pie shell, prebaked (recipe follows, or use your favorite pie crust mix)
2 cups milk, scalded and cooled
5 eggs, beaten with salt and pepper
Fresh or dried oregano or basil to taste (optional)
1 cup grated Cheddar cheese

Preheat oven to 400°F.

Sauté green pepper and onion in oil in a large skillet until just tender. Add salt and pepper to taste. Spread mixture in a prebaked pie shell.

Combine milk and beaten eggs and pour over onion and pepper mixture. Sprinkle with optional herbs and top with grated cheese.

Place pie pan on a cookie sheet and bake at 400°F for 5 minutes. Reduce heat to 325° and bake for 45 minutes, or until firm. (A knife inserted in the center will come out clean when pie is done). Cool 10 minutes before serving.

PIE CRUST

This short-crust pastry makes enough for one 9- to 10-inch single crust pie.

1 cup all-purpose flour
¼ teaspoon salt
4 tablespoons unsalted butter, chilled

1½ tablespoons vegetable shortening, chilled
2–3 tablespoons ice water

Sift the flour and salt into a large bowl. Cut the chilled butter and shortening into the flour with a pastry blender or two knives until the mixture resembles coarse meal.

Add the ice water little by little, pressing the pastry together into a ball. When it holds together and has formed a soft dough, wrap and chill for 1 hour before using.

Roll out on a lightly floured surface.

CURRIED ONIONS AND EGGS

Serves four

English in origin and a little old-fashioned, this one is my idea of the quintessential brunch blow-out (it wouldn't be bad for supper either). It's mad, I know, but here it is. The muffins with chutney butter are the coup de grâce.

2 medium onions, halved
4 tablespoons butter
2–3 tablespoons curry powder
  (Sharwood's is a good one)
1½ cups rich chicken broth
Salt
Freshly ground black pepper
1 tablespoon cornstarch
⅔ cup heavy cream

Juice of ½ lemon
Chutney Butter (recipe follows)
  or butter
4 English muffins, halved
8 poached eggs
4–5 slices crisp-fried bacon, well
  drained and crumbled
Snipped chives

Slice onions lengthwise—not too thin, not too thick.

Melt butter over moderate heat in a heavy skillet. Add onion slices and curry powder and sauté until tender, stirring now and then. Add the broth, season with salt and pepper, lower heat a bit, and simmer for 10 minutes.

Dissolve the cornstarch in the cream and stir into the sauce. Simmer for a few more minutes until thickened. Add the lemon juice and taste for seasoning. Keep warm over low heat.

Spread the chutney butter on the muffins and broil until bubbly. Place two muffin halves on individual heated plates. Working quickly, top each half with a poached egg and a generous spoonful of curried onions. Sprinkle with bacon crumbles and snipped chives and serve immediately.

AFTERTHOUGHTS: You may keep poached eggs hot in a bowl of very warm water. When you need them, remove them with a slotted spoon and blot with a tea towel, taking care not to break the yolks.

This recipe also works well and is greatly simplified by using 6 or 8 hard-boiled eggs, peeled and quartered. Simply place the quartered eggs in a buttered, ovenproof dish, pour the sauce over them, cover dish loosely with foil, and heat through in a 350°F oven. Serve as above.

Try using leeks in place of onions.

How about rolling up the hard-boiled egg mixture in scallion crêpes?

CHUTNEY BUTTER

About 1/2 cup

Soften 8 tablespoons butter and stir in about 3 tablespoons of your favorite brand of chutney. If you come across any large pieces of fruit, chop them. Store, refrigerated, in a covered container.

STUFFED ONIONS

Stuffed onions can be a worthy entrée, a vegetable course, or a handsome garnish. You'll find the general instructions below. Experiment; they're not at all hard to prepare, and the variations are infinite.

Choose Spanish, white, or sweet red onions, and gather together as many as you need. Use the very large ones for entrées, medium-size for side dishes, smallish ones to hold fillings or sauces for garnishes.

Cut a slice off the root end so they will stand alone. Now cut a flat slice from the top. Peel. With a very sharp paring knife, cut a cone shape into the center of each onion body. Then, using a melon-ball cutter or a teaspoon, hollow out the inside, leaving about 3/8 inch of flesh on sides and bottom. Take care not to pierce the bottom or your filling will leak out. Save the corings to chop and sauté as part of the stuffing mixture.

Blanch the onion shells in a pot of gently boiling salted water until firm but tender, 5 to 8 minutes, depending on size and variety. Drain upside down and cool.

Pour a bit of olive oil in your palm, rub your hands together and lightly oil the outside of each onion. Fill the shells with stuffing and place them in a pan just large enough to hold them comfortably. Pour a little water into the bottom of the pan to keep them from scorching, and bake in a preheated 375°F oven until tender, 30 to 40 minutes, depending on size.

Now, a few words on fillings:

Anything you can stuff into a bell pepper or tomato will probably be terrific in an onion shell. Also try them with your favorite meat loaf mixture, tamale pie filling, or poultry stuffing (dare I suggest Stove Top Stuffing?).

Here are a few other ideas:

Seasoned bread crumbs, sautéed ground turkey, onion, etc., held together with a beaten egg and a little cream.

Sautéed onions, frozen drained chopped spinach, feta cheese, nutmeg, egg, and cream.

Shrimp Ball Curry (page 179).

Spinach, beaten egg, cheese, herbs, and bread crumbs.

Sautéed onions, mushrooms, ham, and cheese.

Sausage (try turkey sausage), onions, bread crumbs, mushrooms, etc., and an egg on top.

Sautéed onions, ground lamb, garlic, herbs, pistachios, tomato paste, and beaten egg.

Scallions, creamed spinach, leftover ham or crumbled bacon.

Onion, garlic, and ground beef sautéed together with dill, cooked rice, Sauce Diable (supermarket), and pine nuts.

Vietnamese Tomato stuffing mixture (page 179).

Creamed spinach in the bottom of the shell, a raw egg on the spinach, a spoonful or two of cream. Serve with your best hollandaise, and a sprinkling of chives. An edible ramekin!

Sautéed onions and garlic, a little meat or prosciutto, tomato pulp, pitted black olives, fresh herbs, and olive oil. Cook down to a thick sauce. Spoon into the onion shells and top with cheese. Pizza in an onion.

Quiche fillings.

Poultry stuffing, oysters, and a dash of sherry.

Any leftover meat or poultry, minced and sautéed with onions, garlic, mushrooms, and herbs, and mixed with a beaten egg. Melt cheese over the tops.

Got the idea?

STUFFED ONIONS, CUBAN STYLE

Serves six or seven

Once you get the hang of doing onions like this you will vary the fillings endlessly. It's ideal for leftovers—beef, chicken, or pork. Or try it with drained canned tuna. I have even made a filling of mashed potatoes and cheese. The recipe described here is really only a road map. Experiment!

THE ONIONS

8 large oval-shaped onions   *Beef or chicken broth to cover*

Peel and cut off stem and root ends of onions. Make one careful vertical slit halfway through to the center.

In a saucepan, bring the broth to a boil. Add the onions, reduce heat, and simmer 15 to 20 minutes, or until they are tender enough to separate into layers. Be sure there is enough broth to keep them covered. When they are ready, remove them with a slotted spoon and allow to cool enough to handle. Reserve the broth for another use.

PICADILLO STUFFING

1 cup chopped onion

2 tablespoons olive oil

½ pound each ground beef and pork

1 cup chopped cored, seeded, and drained tomatoes

1 can (4 ounces) mild green chilies, drained

¼ cup chopped, drained pimientos

½ cup raisins

½ cup coarsely chopped pimiento-stuffed olives

2 garlic cloves, minced

1 tablespoon cider vinegar

2 tablespoons tomato paste

¼ teaspoon ground cinnamon

Pinch of ground cloves

Salt

Freshly ground black pepper

In a large skillet sauté the chopped onion in the olive oil over moderate heat until softened. Add beef and pork and cook the mixture, stirring frequently, until the meat is no longer pink. Add the remaining ingredients and cook for 10 minutes, stirring occasionally, until the excess liquid is evaporated, but the mixture is still moist. Taste for seasonings, and adjust as needed.

Assemble the rolls by placing a heaping tablespoon or more of the filling into each onion skin and rolling it closed. (Hold obstinate rolls together with a toothpick.) As the onion rolls will be cooked in batches, you may wish to assemble one batch while you cook another.

FINISHING THE ONIONS

Olive oil	*Paprika*
Butter	*Fresh parsley, minced*
Brown sugar	

Heat 2 tablespoons olive oil and 1 tablespoon butter in a large heavy skillet. Add 1 teaspoon brown sugar and stir until melted. Add the first batch of onions (6 or 8 rolls), seam side down, and sauté slowly over low heat until evenly browned, adding more oil and butter as needed. Turn them when necessary while cooking, and baste often with the glaze in the pan. Remove the browned onions and any pan juices to a gratin dish and keep warm in a low oven.

Repeat the above procedure, using more oil, butter, and brown sugar for each batch, until all the onion rolls are browned. Sprinkle with paprika and minced parsley and serve at once.

AFTERTHOUGHTS: Do try Picadillo Stuffing in cabbage rolls, in whole pimientos, or in green peppers. Stuff it into zucchinis that have been hollowed out and blanched; sprinkle with bread crumbs and Parmesan cheese just before baking.

Why not roll the mixture into balls and sauté? Try them in a good, clear soup with a garnish of chopped chives, cilantro leaves, and a thin slice of lemon.

Picadillo is wonderful in flag-folded filo dough for hors d'oeuvres, too.

Don't forget to omit the brown sugar when using tuna in the filling.

ONION ROASTED TURKEY BREAST WITH PAN GRAVY

Allow about 1/3 pound per serving

Here is the delicious reason for the gravy.

Loosen the skin of the turkey breast and slip a few sprigs of fresh tarragon under it here and there. Pat the meat dry with paper towels. Season to taste with salt and freshly ground pepper and rub it liberally with softened butter. Slice 2 or 3 large onions and place them in a small roaster. Place the turkey on this fragrant bed, and roast it in a moderate (325°F) oven until it's done, basting often with wine or broth. Figure approximately 20 minutes per pound, or consult your butcher.

Serve with Pan Gravy (recipe follows) and, of course, mashed potatoes.

AFTERTHOUGHT: Now, if you choose to make the gravy in the roasting pan, by all means leave the onions in to add their flavor, but the presentation will be nicer if you strain them out before finishing the sauce.

HOW TO MAKE A FINE GRAVY FOR ROAST CHICKEN OR A ROASTED TURKEY BREAST

Much like beurre blanc—not quite as rich, but then again there's more of it.

4 shallots, chopped
⅓ cup white wine vinegar
⅔ cup white wine
1 teaspoon dried tarragon
2 cups chicken broth (the canned
   stuff will do nicely)

3½ tablespoons flour kneaded
   together with 3 tablespoons
   unsalted butter (beurre manié,
   if you care what it's called)
Wedge of lemon
Salt
Freshly ground black pepper
¼ cup heavy cream (optional)

Skim all but 1 tablespoon of the fat from the pan juices in the roasting pan, add the shallots, and cook them over moderate heat until they are softened, stirring frequently.

Add the vinegar, wine, and tarragon and deglaze the pan over moderately high heat, scraping up all the brown bits. Reduce the mixture by half; this is *important.* Add the stock and bring to a boil.

Perfectionists would strain the sauce at this point, but I confess that I hardly ever do. Anyhow, now is the time to stir in the flour–butter mixture, bit by bit, incorporating each addition before adding the next, until the sauce is thickened. Add the salt and pepper to taste, and a squeeze of lemon. Simmer the sauce for 5 minutes. Serve hot, hot.

If you wish to add the optional cream, beat it in a spoonful at a time before the final simmering. Do not allow to boil.

CHICKEN LIVERS WITH SWEET ONIONS

Serves four

These livers are as unexpectedly delicious as they are different. Flavored with long-simmered onions, sherry vinegar, and a hint of anchovy, they make a remarkable first course or a memorable entrée.

1 pound chicken livers, trimmed and halved
Salt
1 cup milk
4 tablespoons butter
4 tablespoons vegetable oil
3 pounds Spanish onions, thinly sliced
2 ounces anchovy fillets, drained

2 teaspoons sugar
½ cup sherry wine vinegar
Freshly ground black pepper
Flour
1 large garlic clove, minced
½ cup strong chicken broth
Finely minced fresh parsley
Fresh chives, cut into ¼-inch lengths

Soak livers in salted milk for 1 hour.

Preheat oven to 325°F.

Melt 2 tablespoons of the butter with 2 tablespoons of the oil in a heavy ovenproof casserole over medium heat. Add onions, tossing to coat with butter and oil, cover tightly, and cook in the preheated oven 2 hours.

Mash anchovies; combine with onions, re-cover, and cook 30 minutes.

Meanwhile, combine sugar with 1/4 cup of the vinegar in a small saucepan over high heat, stirring constantly until sugar dissolves. Add to onions at the end of the 30-minute cooking period. Continue cooking, covered, another 30 minutes. At the end of the last cooking period, the onions should be a rich golden brown. Remove from the oven and set them aside while you prepare the livers; adjust seasonings if necessary.

Drain the livers and pat dry with paper towels. Dust lightly with flour, shaking off any excess.

In a large heavy skillet, melt remaining butter and oil together over moderately high heat. Sauté chicken livers until lightly brown and just cooked through, leaving them tinged pink inside. Add garlic the last minute or so of sautéing.

While livers are sautéing, transfer onions to a heated serving dish and keep warm. When livers are done, place them on the serving dish with the onions and keep warm while you prepare the sauce.

Deglaze the pan with the remaining vinegar, scraping up any clinging brown bits. Add broth, stirring, and reduce to a syrupy glaze. Drizzle this glaze over the livers and onions. Sprinkle with fresh herbs and serve immediately.

AFTERTHOUGHT: Thinly sliced Bruschetta (page 64) or toasted French bread would go nicely with the livers.

SWORDFISH MÉDITERRANÉE

Serves four

A vivid dish that tastes as good as it looks, and may be served hot or at room temperature.

*1½ pounds swordfish, cut into
  2-inch chunks
6 tablespoons fruity olive oil
¼ cup dry white wine
Few sprigs of fresh thyme, or ½
  teaspoon dried
4 medium sweet onions, chopped
1 pound unpeeled tomatoes,
  cored, chopped, and drained
3 garlic cloves, minced*

*1 teaspoon fresh oregano leaves,
  or ½ teaspoon dried
2 strips orange peel, 2 to 3
  inches long
Salt
Freshly ground black pepper
10 oil-cured black olives
1 roasted sweet red pepper, cored,
  seeded, and sliced into strips
1 roasted green pepper, cored,
  seeded, and sliced into strips*

Put the swordfish chunks in a bowl with 2 tablespoons of the olive oil, the wine, and thyme, and let them absorb the marinade for an hour or two.

Preheat the oven to 375°F.

Heat a little of the remaining olive oil in a pan and soften the onions. Add the tomatoes, garlic, oregano, orange peel, salt, and pepper. Bring to a boil, lower heat, and simmer for about 15 minutes.

Spoon the fish and its marinade into an ovenproof dish, pour the onion-tomato mixture over it, mix it around a bit, and bake for 30 minutes. Serve hot or warm garnished with the olives and peppers and drizzled with remaining olive oil.

AFTERTHOUGHTS: This dish is usually served with triangles of white bread that have been fried—deadly, but good.

If fresh tomatoes don't look good, use drained canned ones.

CRISPY ONION TROUT

Serves two

Finished with crisp hot chilies and onions, sweet fresh trout never tasted better!

2 whole trout, each about 1 pound, cleaned	*1 medium onion, halved and sliced thin*
Sherry	*1 green chili, minced, or more to taste*
Dark soy sauce	
½ cup mild vegetable oil	*6 tablespoons light soy sauce*

Wipe fish with damp paper towels, then pat dry. Make 3 or 4 diagonal slashes on both sides of fish and rinse with sherry and dark soy sauce. Place trout on a plate.

Set plate on a steaming rack over boiling water. Cover and steam 15 minutes, or until just cooked through and tender.

Five minutes before the fish is cooked, heat the oil in a small pan. Brown onion and chili until crispy and very dark. Add light soy sauce and let splatter die down. Turn off heat.

Remove fish from steamer and pour sauce over them. Serve hot with steamed rice and curried vegetables.

AFTERTHOUGHT: This dish is glorious using shallots in place of the onions. Prepare as above.

MATELOTE À LA NORMANDE

Serves eight

A classic dish from Normandy, matelote is simple to make and takes very little time. It may be made with red or white wine and any single kind of fish or a mixture. Serve it with Bruschetta (page 64), Croutons (page 67), or a lot of crusty bread. Vive la France!

2 pounds boneless white fish (halibut, snapper, monk fish, or any other that looks good to you)

2 pounds tightly closed mussels (the New Zealand ones are best)

6 tablespoons butter

3 onions, chopped fine

1 fat garlic clove, minced

1½ cups rosé wine or a full-bodied white

¼ cup flour

A few shrimp, cooked and shelled

2 tablespoons minced fresh parsley

Fresh lemon juice

Salt

Freshly ground black pepper

1 tablespoon snipped chives

Cut the fish into large chunks. Reserve.

Scrub the mussels well, remove the beards, and put them in a large saucepan with 1/4 cup water. Cover the pan and shake it over a fierce fire until the mussels open, 3 or 4 minutes. Strain the liquid into a bowl and set aside. Allow the mussels to cool, shell them, and discard any whose shells did not open.

In another large saucepan heat 2 tablespoons of the butter. Add the onions and garlic and sauté them until tender but not brown. Add the liquid from the mussels, the wine, and the chunks of fish, which should be covered by the liquid. If not, add water just to cover. Simmer gently until the fish is just cooked, 5 to 8 minutes.

Work the flour and remaining 4 tablespoons butter together and add it to the simmering liquid. Allow it to dissolve, stirring gently as it thickens, 3 to 4 minutes.

Add the mussels, shrimp, and parsley. Taste for seasoning and, if you think it needs it, add the lemon juice and salt, and pepper.

Heat just long enough to warm the shellfish. Don't overdo this or they'll toughen. Serve at once in deep, warm soup bowls garnished with chives.

❦

BLANQUETTE DE VEAU

Serves six

This delicious, luxurious, and tender dish is Wolfgang Puck's inspired version of the classic French dish. And I can tell you from experience that it may well be the food of love. Once upon a time I made it for a friend of mine to serve to her hero in an afternoon of dalliance. On parting he asked her to prepare it for him again on his next visit. Now I ask you, did I have her in my power or not?

2–3 tablespoons mild vegetable oil

3 pounds boneless veal stew meat, cut into 1-inch cubes

3 tablespoons butter

1 large onion, minced

6 carrots, chopped

1 stalk celery, chopped

3 tablespoons flour

2 cups dry white wine

3 cups chicken broth

Bouquet garni (a few sprigs of parsley, some thyme, and a small bay leaf tied together in cheesecloth)

Salt

Freshly ground pepper

1 cup cream

Lemon juice

1 stalk broccoli, stem removed, separated into tiny florets

Fresh parsley, minced

Heat oil in a large, heavy saucepan. Sauté veal cubes until evenly golden brown (do not overbrown), removing them to a plate as they finish. Discard the oil. In the same saucepan, melt butter and sauté onion, carrots, and celery until the onion is translucent.

Return meat to the pan. Sprinkle with flour, stirring well to combine. Deglaze pan with white wine and bring to a boil.

Add broth, bouquet garni, and salt and pepper to taste. Simmer slowly until meat is tender, 1 to 1 1/2 hours.

Transfer meat to another saucepan. Add cream to the cooking liquid and reduce until thickened. Strain sauce over meat, bring to a boil, and season to taste with lemon juice. Add more salt and pepper if needed. Keep warm over a low flame.

Blanch broccoli florets in boiling water until barely tender, approximately 2 minutes. Drain.

Transfer blanquette to a heated deep serving platter. Garnish with broccoli and parsley.

AFTERTHOUGHTS: Rice pilaf would be a nice accompaniment. This would be lovely with tiny boiling onions that have been blanched, peeled, and sautéed in butter until golden. Add them to the strained sauce and veal.

Or, use 18–20 peeled, roasted shallots. Oil them lightly and roast till brown, then add them to the strained sauce and veal.

VEAL STEW WITH ONIONS

8 to 10 servings

A satisfying dish with or without an afternoon's dalliance.

*3 pounds boneless veal stew
   meat, cut into 1-inch cubes*
Best olive oil
¼ cup flour
10–12 garlic cloves, chopped
3 cups chicken broth
*1½ cups dry vermouth or white
   wine*

*1 tablespoon chopped fresh
   rosemary*
1 teaspoon chopped fresh oregano
Salt
Freshly ground black pepper
2 pounds white pearl onions
Minced parsley
Chopped chives

Dry veal cubes with paper towels.

In a heavy ovenproof casserole, heat olive oil over moderately high heat and brown veal cubes, several at a time, transferring them to a bowl as they are done. Add more oil as necessary.

Preheat oven to 325°F.

When all the veal is browned, sprinkle with flour and toss to coat evenly. Set aside.

Briefly sauté the garlic in the olive oil; remove with a slotted spoon. Pour off all the fat from the casserole and add the garlic and chicken broth, deglazing the pan while scraping up all the brown bits that may be clinging to the sides and bottom. Add wine, rosemary, oregano, salt and black pepper to taste, the veal, and bring to a boil. Cover and place casserole in the preheated oven for 1 hour, stirring occasionally.

Cut a shallow X in the root end of each onion. Drop them into a large pot of boiling salted water and cook until barely tender, about 15 minutes. Drain; drop them into cold water to cool. Drain again, slip off their skins, and set aside.

At the end of the 1-hour cooking time, add the onions to the veal, stir, and cook for another 20 minutes, uncovering the casserole for the last 10 minutes. Taste for seasonings, sprinkle with parsley and chives, and serve.

VEALTAILS WITH ORANGE AND WALNUTS

Serves six

"Remember this, daughter, skimpy meals make mean men." When my father dropped that one on me he must have had a dish like this in mind. Slyly designed to nourish body and soul and please the eye, it holds many surprises and layers of tastes. When you serve this one, you will cosset your friends and calm their restless hearts. A reverent silence usually ensues.

THE VEALTAILS

3½ pounds vealtails, cut in 2-inch pieces (Do look for these. They are tender and delicate, and well worth the search. See Afterthoughts.)
Flour
⅓ cup peanut oil
2 large yellow onions, halved and thinly sliced
6 garlic cloves, finely chopped
1 cup dry red wine

1 cup tomato purée (Pomi is excellent)
2 cups strong beef broth (homemade or improved canned)
Juice of 1 orange and its rind, quartered
Salt
Freshly ground black pepper
1 teaspoon herbes de Provence

THE ONIONS

2 dozen small white onions, 1½
  to 2 inches in diameter,
  blanched and peeled
¼ cup peanut oil
1 cup dry red wine
½ cup dry sherry or Madeira

1 heaping tablespoon brown
  sugar
¼ cup balsamic vinegar
Salt
Freshly ground black pepper
Lump of unsalted butter

THE WALNUTS

¼ cup walnut or peanut oil

¾ cup walnuts, coarsely chopped

THE ORANGE GLAZE

Peel of 1 orange, cut into
  julienne

⅓ cup red wine vinegar
1 tablespoon brown sugar

GARNISH

Minced parsley

Chopped pickled jalapeño peppers

To prepare the vealtails, remove any excess fat and drop them into a large paper bag with a handful or two of flour. Shake to coat.

In a large heavy sauté pan, heat peanut oil over moderate heat. Shake off any excess flour from meat and add it to the pan; brown slowly. Take your time with this step; slow browning equals deep flavor. If your pan is not large enough to hold all the meat at once, cook it in batches. Transfer the finished meat to a plate and reserve. Discard all but 2 tablespoons of oil.

Add onions and garlic to the pan and sauté until softened and just beginning to color. Do not brown. Stir in the red wine, raise the heat, and deglaze the pan, scraping up any brown bits. Add the tomato purée, beef broth, orange juice and rind, salt and pepper to taste, herbes de Provence, and the reserved vealtails. Stir well, lower heat to simmer, cover, and cook slowly 2 1/2 to 3 hours, or until meat is tender and the sauce has thickened. Stir occasionally to keep from sticking. Turn off heat and allow to mellow at least 2 hours, or, preferably, refrigerated overnight.

TO PREPARE THE ONIONS

Preheat oven to 400°F.

Sauté white onions in peanut oil until lightly browned, shaking pan occasionally to keep them moving. Don't worry, they will not color evenly. Transfer onions to a shallow casserole just large enough to hold them in one layer. Pour off oil.

Add wine, sherry, brown sugar, balsamic vinegar, salt and pepper to taste, and the lump of butter; cook, stirring, until the sauce reduces and thickens a bit. Pour the sauce over the onions and bake them for about 45 minutes, basting and turning them occasionally, until brown and tender when pierced with a fork. Set aside.

TO PREPARE THE WALNUTS

Heat walnut oil in a small, heavy skillet over medium heat. Add walnuts and stir frequently until brown and crispy. Drain them on paper towels and set aside.

TO PREPARE THE ORANGE GLAZE

Combine the orange peel, wine, and brown sugar in a small saucepan. Cook over medium-high heat, stirring constantly, until reduced and syrupy. Reserve.

TO ASSEMBLE THE RAGOUT

Skim any fat that may have risen to the surface of the casserole.

Add onions and heat veal slowly over a low-moderate flame, stirring occasionally.

Transfer vealtails and onions to a large heated serving platter, if desired. Spoon glaze over them (add a bit of the hot sauce to the glaze and stir if it has hardened). Garnish with toasted walnuts and minced parsley and serve immediately, accompanied by a small dish of chopped pickled jalapeños.

AFTERTHOUGHTS: If you cannot find vealtails, you may successfully substitute veal shanks (sawed into 2-inch pieces as for osso buco), or lamb shanks (similarly), or, last resort, oxtails (about 4 1/2 pounds in 2- to 3-inch pieces).

The ragout goes nicely with bow tie noodles, orzo (ricelike pasta), hot riced potatoes, or, of course, mashed potatoes. Accompany with a simple green salad, crusty French or Italian bread, and a lusty Zinfandel.

MEDALLIONS OF VEAL WITH ONION MARMALADE

Serves four

Elegant and simple; Wolf scores again! Perfect for wooing titans of industry, and treasured companions.

2 large onions, cut into eighths
1 teaspoon salt
Freshly ground black pepper
2 cups chicken broth
1 tablespoon good red or sherry
    wine vinegar
1 cup heavy cream
1½ pounds veal loin, sliced into
    8 medallions, 3 ounces each

1 tablespoon all-purpose flour
2 tablespoons unsalted butter
1 tablespoon mild-flavored oil
½ cup port
Onion Marmalade, Wolfgang
    Puck (recipe follows)

Season the onions with 1/2 teaspoon of the salt and pepper to taste. In a medium saucepan, combine 1 1/2 cups of the broth, the vinegar, and the onions. Cover pan and cook over moderate heat until liquid has evaporated, about 15 minutes.

In a small saucepan, reduce the cream until 3 tablespoons remain. Add the cream to the onions and bring to a boil. Remove onions from heat and keep warm.

Season the veal with the remaining 1/2 teaspoon salt and pepper to taste. Dust lightly with the flour. Heat a heavy skillet and add 1/2 tablespoon of the butter and the 1 tablespoon oil. Sauté the medallions until golden brown on both sides but still pink inside (3 or 4 minutes on each side). Transfer to a heated platter and keep warm.

Pour grease from the skillet and deglaze with port. Add the remaining 1/2 cup broth and reduce until 3 tablespoons remain. Slowly whisk in the remaining 1 1/2 tablespoons butter.

Arrange onions on each serving plate, top with two veal medallions, and lightly nap with sauce. Serve with onion marmalade.

ONION MARMALADE, WOLFGANG PUCK

About 3 cups

This suave onion marmalade is one of the many, many innovative dishes I learned to make while working with the gifted, endlessly imaginative chef Wolfgang Puck. Wolf serves this savory concoction with medallions of veal. If the price of medallions brings visions of imminent insolvency to your mind (as it does to mine), let me reassure you that this marmalade will lift a simple paillard of chicken to new heights, or lend itself happily to a boned pork chop or smoked tongue—and that's just for starters.

2 large or 3 medium onions, cut into eighths
½ teaspoon salt
Freshly ground black pepper

1½ cups chicken broth
1 tablespoon good red or sherry wine vinegar
1 cup heavy cream

Season the onions with salt and pepper to taste. Put the broth, the vinegar, and the onions in a medium saucepan. Cover the pan and cook over moderate heat until the liquid has evaporated, about 15 minutes.

In a small saucepan, reduce the cream until 3 tablespoons remain. Add the cream to the onions and bring to a boil. Remove from the heat and reserve in a warm place until ready to serve.

AFTERTHOUGHT: Do try the marmalade with pork tenderloin, grilled or braised.

MOROCCAN CAMMAMA
(Spiced Lamb with Onions)

Serves four to six

If you're feeling rich and powerful, take a quantum leap and make this exotic dish with sweet Vidalia onions. It's an order of magnitude better.

3 tablespoons olive oil

2½ pounds boneless lamb
  shoulder, trimmed and cut
  into 1-inch pieces

1 large onion, chopped

1 teaspoon ground cinnamon

¼ teaspoon ground ginger

½ teaspoon toasted cumin seeds,
  crushed

Pinch of saffron threads,
  crumbled

1 teaspoon crushed dried red
  chilies

2 large garlic cloves, minced

¼ cup chopped fresh cilantro

Salt

Freshly ground black pepper

2 strips orange peel, about 3
  inches long

2 tablespoons honey

3 lemons

Chicken broth or water

6 large yellow onions, halved
  and sliced into crescents

Sprigs of fresh cilantro

Heat the olive oil in a large casserole over medium heat. Add the lamb and chopped onion and sauté 5 minutes, stirring frequently. Add the cinnamon, ginger, cumin, saffron, chilies, garlic, cilantro, salt, pepper, orange peel, honey, juice of 1 lemon, and enough chicken broth or water to just cover ingredients. Cover the casserole and simmer very slowly 2 hours, stirring occasionally.

Add the yellow onions, stir well, cover, and simmer 20 minutes, or until onions are just tender.

Preheat oven to 425°F.

With a slotted spoon, transfer ingredients to a large bowl. Raise heat to high and reduce liquid by half. Add juice of the remaining lemons, stirring well. Return ingredients to casserole, stir until blended, taste for seasonings, and place in the preheated oven, uncovered. When the top of the cammama is slightly glazed, serve immediately, garnished with a few sprigs of cilantro, and accompanied by rice, Date and Onion Sambal (page 119), a salad of diced cucumbers and ripe tomatoes dressed with oil, vinegar, and salt, and a basket of warm pita bread.

AFTERTHOUGHT: You may substitute boned chicken thighs for the lamb if you wish.

CALF'S TONGUE BRAISED WITH ONIONS AND RED WINE

Serves six

Here is another of Wolf's inspired dishes. It's inexpensive, low in calories, satisfying, *and* uses lots of onions and garlic.

*2 calves' tongues, approximately
  2 pounds
2 cups red wine (such as Petit
  Sirah)
2 cups chicken broth
2 pounds onions, sliced thin
1 tablespoon good red or sherry
  wine vinegar
3 medium tomatoes, peeled,
  seeded, and diced*

*1 stalk celery, sliced
1 small bay leaf
Pinch of dried thyme
2 garlic cloves, unpeeled
Sprig of fresh tarragon
Salt
Freshly ground black pepper
1 tablespoon minced fresh
  tarragon*

In a large saucepan, cook the tongues in boiling salted water for 45 minutes. Refresh under cold running water and peel if possible. If the tongues do not peel easily, continue the recipe and peel just before slicing.

Preheat oven to 400°F.

In a saucepan, reduce the wine to 1 cup, add the broth, and heat through.

Place the tongues in an ovenproof casserole. Top with onions, vinegar, tomatoes, celery, bay leaf, thyme, garlic, and tarragon sprig. Cover and cook in the oven for approximately 1 hour, or until tender. As the liquid reduces, add a bit more broth or water, if necessary, to prevent burning.

Remove the tongues from the casserole and keep warm. Transfer the vegetables to a food processor or blender and purée. Reheat. Season with salt and pepper to taste.

Slice the tongues and cover each serving with sauce. Sprinkle with minced tarragon. A light red wine such as St. Emilion goes well with this dish.

SMOKED TONGUE WITH TRIPLE ONIONS

Serves six to eight

Tender and delectable, the tongue is simmered under an aromatic blanket of onions, leeks, and garlic, and is served with tiny caramelized white onions.

1 smoked calf's tongue, 2 to 2½ pounds
1 large onion stuck with 3 cloves
1 celery rib with leaves
Peppercorns
4 tablespoons butter
2 leeks, white part only, well washed and trimmed, sliced into ½-inch rounds
2 medium onions, halved and cut into lengthwise slices
10 garlic cloves, blanched 3 minutes and peeled

2 tablespoons fresh thyme leaves, or 2 teaspoons dried thyme, crumbled
2 tablespoons fresh lemon juice
2 teaspoons grated lemon peel
1 tablespoon Dijon mustard
1 cup full-bodied dry red wine
Caramelized Onions (recipe follows)
Few sprigs of fresh thyme or watercress

Wash the tongue well. Place it in a large saucepan with the clove-studded onion, the celery rib, and a few peppercorns. Cover with water and bring to a boil. Reduce heat and simmer about 1 hour, or until tender when pierced with a fork. Remove tongue; discard boiling liquid. Refresh the tongue under cold running water until cool enough to handle. Skin and trim, and set aside.

Preheat oven to 350°F.

Melt the butter in a heavy skillet over medium heat. Sauté the leeks, onions, and garlic, stirring occasionally, until they are softened and just beginning to color, about 15 minutes.

Add the thyme, lemon juice, peel, and mustard and mix well. Pour in the wine and simmer until the mixture is reduced slightly and the wine has mellowed. Remove from heat.

Slice the tongue on the diagonal about 1/2 inch thick and arrange in a single overlapping layer in a buttered ovenproof casserole. Pour the onion mixture over the slices and cover loosely with foil. Place in the preheated oven for 45 minutes to 1 hour.

At the end of the cooking time, place the tongue and its onion mixture on a heated platter. Surround the tongue and onions with caramelized onions and garnish with a few sprigs of fresh thyme or watercress.

AFTERTHOUGHTS: You may also like to try this dish using chicken pieces. If so, use dry white wine, vermouth, or 1 1/2 cups chicken broth. Brown the chicken lightly in oil before baking.

How about using center-cut pork chops?

CARAMELIZED ONIONS

3 tablespoons butter	3 tablespoons brown sugar
3 tablespoons olive oil	¼ cup sherry wine vinegar
2 pounds small white boiling	¼ cup dry sherry wine
onions, blanched and peeled	Salt

Melt butter and olive oil in a large heavy skillet over medium-low heat. Add onions, sprinkle with sugar, and cook until the onions are softened and light golden in color, about 30 minutes. Stir frequently while cooking.

Increase the heat and add the vinegar, cooking until it is reduced by half. Reduce the heat to medium-low, and add the sherry and a pinch of salt. Simmer until the onions are caramelized and the juices are syrupy, stirring occasionally, about 10 minutes. Serve hot or lukewarm to accompany roast or grilled meat or chicken, and, of course, smoked tongue.

RAGOUT OF SAUSAGES WITH SMALL ONIONS

Serves six

One rainy spring evening I served this dish to some hungry friends along with a crusty loaf of sourdough to mop up the sauce. We started off with a salad of fresh asparagus on a bed of small spinach leaves beribboned with a gorgeous raspberry vinaigrette, and wound up the feast with a sorbet of fresh strawberries, which I had run up in my trusty little machine. We all felt better for it, too, the slings and arrows of outrageous fortune held at bay once more.

1 cotechino sausage (see Afterthoughts)	1½ cups beef or chicken broth
6 Italian sausages	3 tablespoons balsamic vinegar
2 tablespoons butter	2 tablespoons tomato paste
2 pounds small white onions, peeled	1 scant teaspoon crushed dried red chilies
6 bratwurst, halved	Salt
1 tablespoon flour	Freshly ground black pepper
1½ cups beer	Fresh parsley and chives, chopped

Simmer the cotechino, casing and all, in water to cover for 30 minutes. Drain, cool, remove casing, and slice into sixths.

Meanwhile preheat oven to 400°F. Make three slashes with a sharp knife in each Italian sausage. Place them in a baking pan and roast them in the oven for 15 to 20 minutes, or until crisp and brown. (If you line the baking pan with foil, the cleanup will be a cinch.) Drain and set aside.

Heat the butter in heavy skillet or sauté pan. When it is frothy, add the peeled onions and sauté them gently, shaking the pan now and then. When they begin to take on a little color, watch them carefully; the color changes faster now. When they are a rich, golden brown, remove them from the pan and reserve. Add the bratwurst and roll them around in the pan to lightly brown. Set aside. Pour off all but 1 tablespoon fat.

Sprinkle the flour into the pan and stir it around, scraping up any brown bits that lurk there. When the flour has colored, stir in the beer, broth, vinegar, tomato paste, and chilies and let it boil up. Over a brisk fire, allow the sauce to cook merrily until it is reduced by nearly half and is shiny and slightly thickened. Taste for seasoning. Now is the time to add anything you think it needs—salt and pepper, a little shot of Tabasco, perhaps?

Return all the sausages and onions to the pan. Baste them with the sauce, lower the heat, put the lid on the pan, and let them simmer together for a few minutes. At that point you can turn off the fire and allow the ragout to mellow until you're ready to serve it. Skim off any fat before you do.

Transfer the ragout to a heated deep serving platter. Garnish with chopped parsley and chives. Serve with polenta (outstanding), noodles, boiled or mashed potatoes, or just some good, crusty bread.

AFTERTHOUGHTS: Cotechino is a succulent pork sausage, available in Italian markets. About 3 inches in diameter, it comes in a casing and usually weights about 1 1/2 pounds. Cotechino is subtly seasoned with wine and spices and adds a lot to this dish. It also makes a splendid entrée simmered, sliced, and served on a bed of sautéed spinach, accompanied by a light mustard sauce or simply a fine spicy mustard. It's worth searching out. I think you'll enjoy it.

This ragout may be made with a variety of sausages: smoked Pennsylvanias, Louisiana hot links, English pork sausages (bangers), or Polish kielbasas. The mild veal sausages such as bratwurst and bockwurst absorb the delicious flavors of the savory brown sauce. My favorites are hot, spicy Portuguese sausages, but, then again, the rich flavor of the French ones also combine beautifully with the other sausages in this lusty, oniony ragout. Try some improvisations of your own with contrasting textures, seasonings, and shapes.

I don't see why this dish wouldn't be good made with brown onions if the silver ones aren't available. Peel them, halve them from stem to root, slice 1/3 inch thick, and proceed.

I think the ragout would be just as good if you skipped the beer altogether and substituted apple cider, a shot of Calvados, and, perhaps, a dash of vinegar.

PORK CHOPS WITH ONIONS
AND PRUNES

Serves six

I once lived in a wonderful old building that had been a church. The place was always filled with people—especially the kitchen, where my friends gathered, laughing and talking, while I cooked. This is one of the dishes I made to feed them and, incidentally, quiet them down for a while. I served it in a beautiful wooden bowl, the chops and their attendants wreathed with the crisp Chinese peas. A feathery grits soufflé went to the table with the chops. It was always a smash, and I commend it to you.

2 pounds boned pork chops	*Salt*
Flour	*Freshly ground black pepper*
Oil for sauté	*½ lemon*
1 cup dry red wine	*1 cup pitted prunes*
1 cup chicken or beef broth	*1 cup crisp-cooked Chinese pea*
2 garlic cloves, minced	*pods*
1 pound small boiling onions,	
peeled (see Afterthought)	

Dust the chops lightly with flour and brown quickly in hot oil. Remove them to a plate as they finish.

Pour off oil and deglaze the pan with red wine, scraping up any brown bits. Add broth and minced garlic and reduce slightly. Return the chops to the pan and add onions, salt, pepper, and a squeeze of lemon. Cover and simmer 20 to 25 minutes.

Add the prunes, adjust the seasonings, cover, and cook gently for another 10 to 15 minutes, or until the chops are tender and the onions are cooked.

Remove the chops and keep them warm while you reduce the sauce. Arrange them on a warm platter, garnish with the onions and prunes, pour the sauce over all, and top with the crisp Chinese peas.

AFTERTHOUGHT: You may use frozen boiling onions to simplify this recipe. They are uniform in size and peeled. Just defrost them and they're ready to go.

VEGETABLES

BOILED PEARL ONIONS

Serves six to eight

The first step . . .

2 pounds white pearl onions, *Salt*
   unpeeled   *Freshly ground black pepper*

Bring a pan of salted water to a boil. Cut an X into the root end of each onion, being careful not to cut too deep; otherwise they will fall apart during cooking. Drop onions in the water and cook until tender, 12 to 15 minutes. Test with the point of a sharp knife. Drain and plunge into cold water. Drain again.

    When onions are cool enough to handle, peel them. Trim ends neatly. Season with salt and pepper to taste.

CREAMED ONIONS

A nice big bowl of onions in béchamel sauce—suitable for any feast.

4 tablespoons unsalted butter, *Freshly ground black pepper*
   softened   *Freshly grated nutmeg*
6 tablespoons flour   2 pounds white pearl onions,
2 cups milk   *boiled*
Salt

Prepare beurre manié by combining butter and flour in a bowl until well blended.

Bring milk to a boil in a heavy saucepan. When milk begins to boil, whisk in the beurre manié and continue whisking over moderately low heat until smooth and thickened. Add salt and pepper to taste, and a few gratings of nutmeg. Lower heat to a simmer, add onions, and heat through. Serve immediately.

AFTERTHOUGHTS: Add a package of defrosted, drained tiny peas to the creamed onions a couple of minutes before serving.

How about crumbling sausage into the béchamel and serving it over biscuits? Or pouring a tablespoon or so of Worcestershire sauce into the sauce for creamed chipped beef? Just wondering.

ROASTED ONIONS, PLAIN AND SIMPLE

You'll think of many uses for these beauties.

1 large onion per person

Preheat oven to 400°F, or fire up the grill.

Gather as many onions as you need, but don't peel them. If you are baking them, place on a baking sheet in the oven for about an hour. Test them with the point of a sharp knife. No resistance means they're done. If you're going to grill them over the coals, put them skin and all on the rack and turn them frequently; cook until tender and the skin is blackened.

Retrieve them from oven or grill, remove the peels and roots, cut into quarters, and fill them with butter, salt, and pepper. Serve with grilled meat, chicken, or whatever.

ROASTED ONION PURÉE

Try mixing some of this purée into mashed potatoes. It's a dish for the true aficionado.

Follow the instructions for Roasted Onions, and just let them continue cooking until very soft. Then peel, remove roots, and drop them into a blender. Purée to a smooth consistency.

AFTERTHOUGHT: Try mixing mashed potatoes, onion purée, lots of butter and yogurt or sour cream together. Season with salt and pepper. Makes grown men cry.

YORKSHIRE ONIONS

Serves six

A new twist for a couple of old standbys, and a grand accompaniment for roast beef or chicken; in fact, anything that has some gravy.

6–8 medium brown onions, evenly matched	*3–4 teaspoons butter* *Freshly ground black pepper*

Prepare the onion shells as for Stuffed Onions (page 92). When they are just tender, drain them well; you might even pat the insides with paper towels. Put 1/2 teaspoon butter into each shell and a grinding of pepper. Place the shells on a baking sheet and pour into each one the following mixture (make it while the onions are boiling).

3 whole eggs *1 cup milk* *½ teaspoon salt*	*1 cup flour* *6–8 fresh sage leaves*

Preheat oven to 400°F.

Place the eggs in a blender; whirl for a second or two. Add the milk, salt, and flour, and whirl until just blended.

Fill onion shells to the top, push a fresh sage leaf into each one, and bake in the preheated oven for about 35 minutes, or until the tops are nicely brown.

What a treat—the onions become all shiny and sweet, the custardy filling absorbs the sage and onion flavors, and it's just delicious with or without a spoonful of gravy.

ENGLISH ONIONS

4 cups

Serve these tart-sweet onions with roasted or broiled meats and chicken or turkey, as a sambal with curries, or as part of a light lunch or supper of cold cuts, smoked sausages, and cheeses.

1½ cups Madeira
¾ cup red wine vinegar
½ cup brown sugar
½ cup currants or raisins
⅛ teaspoon cayenne pepper

2 pounds tiny whole white
* onions*
¼ cup vegetable oil
Salt

In a large saucepan, combine Madeira, vinegar, sugar, currants, and cayenne pepper. Bring to a boil and cook rapidly until mixture is reduced to 1 1/4 cups. Set aside.

Peel onions (parboil for 1 minute and then slip the skins right off). Heat oil in a large frying pan over medium-high heat. Add enough onions to form a single layer and sauté until lightly browned, shaking pan frequently to turn onions. When well-colored, remove from pan to saucepan with Madeira mixture. Brown remaining onions, adding more oil if necessary, transferring them to the saucepan when finished.

Bring onions and Madeira mixture to a boil, cover, lower heat, and allow to simmer slowly until onions are tender but still slightly crisp inside. Cool. Season with salt to taste.

Store, refrigerated, for 3 to 4 days. Serve at room temperature.

SPICED ONIONS

Serves eight

A piquant accompaniment to your grills and roasts.

2 onions, thinly sliced and separated into rings	*2–3 tablespoons sugar*
6 tablespoons olive oil	*2 tablespoons hot pepper sauce*
¼ cup red wine vinegar	*½ teaspoon salt*

Drop onions into a large pot of boiling water. Turn off heat immediately, count rapidly to 30, and drain them in a colander. Cool them under cold running water and drain thoroughly.

Mix oil, vinegar, sugar, pepper sauce, and salt together in a mixing bowl. Add onions to mixture and stir thoroughly to coat.

Marinate overnight in the refrigerator. Allow to sit at room temperature 1/2 hour before serving.

DATE AND ONION SAMBAL

About 1 3/4 cups

A caprice, this, and quite wonderful with a hot, hot curry.

1 medium onion, halved lengthwise and cut into slivers	*¼ cup red wine vinegar*
8 ounces pitted dates, cut lengthwise into quarters	*½ teaspoon salt*
	½ teaspoon sugar

Combine the onion slivers and dates in a serving bowl.

In a small bowl, whisk together the vinegar, salt, and sugar until the sugar dissolves. Pour over the dates and onions and combine well to coat with marinade.

AFTERTHOUGHT: This sambal will keep for a couple of days, covered tightly and refrigerated.

SCALLOPED ONIONS AND APPLES

Serves six

This is great with pork chops or roast.

1½ pounds yellow onions, peeled
    and chopped
1½ pounds tart apples, peeled,
    cored, and thinly sliced
½ cup brown sugar
½ cup heavy cream
4 tablespoons butter, melted and
    cooled

1 tablespoon lemon juice
½ teaspoon cinnamon
Salt
Cayenne pepper
½ cup fresh bread crumbs

Preheat oven to 350°F.

In a large bowl, combine the onions and apples with the sugar,
cream, butter, lemon juice and seasonings, tossing gently to avoid
breaking the apple slices.

Place the mixture in a well-buttered, 2-quart shallow baking dish.
Bake in the preheated oven for 1 hour.

Sprinkle the top with the bread crumbs and bake for another 30
minutes, or until the crumbs are golden and the apples are tender.

BAKED ONIONS VINAIGRETTE

Serves eight

Familiar ingredients with a nice new twist.

4 tablespoons butter
8 large onions, cut into large
    chunks, soaked 30 minutes in
    ice water, and drained
½ cup uncooked long-grain rice
1 cup grated Gruyère or Swiss
    cheese

⅔ cup half-and-half
Salt
Freshly ground black pepper
1 tablespoon chopped fresh herbs
½ cup Mustard Vinaigrette
    (page 52)

Melt butter in a large skillet over low heat. Add onions and sauté until transparent. Do not allow them to brown. Remove from heat and set aside.

Preheat oven to 325°F.

Cook rice in 3 cups boiling water for 5 minutes; drain well. Add to onions with cheese and half-and-half. Season with salt and pepper to taste and pour into a shallow 2-quart baking/serving dish. Bake 1 hour. Allow to cool to room temperature.

Combine herbs with vinaigrette. Serve on the side for your guests to drizzle over the onions.

CRISP NUTTY BAKED ONIONS

Serves six

A dandy first course or a nice accompaniment for grilled things.

3 very large yellow onions	*2 teaspoons honey*
1 cup chicken broth	*1 teaspoon grated lemon peel*
1 tablespoon butter	*½ teaspoon salt*
¼ teaspoon sweet Hungarian	*Freshly ground black pepper*
* paprika*	*⅓ cup finely chopped pecans*

Preheat oven to 350°F.

Peel the onions and cut them in half crosswise. Place them, cut side up, in a large baking dish.

In a saucepan, combine the broth, butter, paprika, honey, lemon peel, salt, and pepper to taste. Bring to a simmer, then pour the mixture over the onions and bake them, covered, for 50 minutes to 1 hour.

When the onions are tender, sprinkle them with the pecans and bake, uncovered, 10 to 15 minutes, or until the nuts are lightly browned.

RED ONION FLOWERS

Serves six

Remember when we were children and as a special treat were given those pretty little shells to drop into a glass of water? As they opened—wonder of wonders—a brightly colored mermaid's garden appeared, waving gently in the water. These beautiful Red Onion Flowers are almost as much fun to watch as they emerge from their foil packets with petals unfolding—the part of me that's still a child thinks so.

6 red onions (no larger than 3 inches in diameter), peeled
1½ teaspoons balsamic vinegar
6 tablespoons olive oil

6 teaspoons mango chutney
Salt
Freshly ground black pepper

Trim the root end of each onion carefully so that the onion is still intact. Standing each onion on its end, cut parallel vertical slices at 1/4-inch intervals into, but not through, the onion, stopping about 1/2 inch above the root end. Turn each onion 90 degrees and cut parallel vertical slices in the same manner to form a crosshatch pattern, keeping the onions intact. Drop them into a large bowl of ice cubes and cold water and let them soak for 2 to 4 hours, or until they have opened into flowers.

Drain, root end up, for 10 minutes. Place each onion root end down in the center of a square of foil, drizzle with vinegar, 1 tablespoon of oil, and 1 teaspoon of mango chutney. Season the onions with salt and pepper.

Bring the edges of the foil together to enclose the onions, crimping the edges to seal them. Grill the packets over glowing coals for 30 to 45 minutes.

To serve, remove from foil and allow flowers to unfold on a serving platter or individual plates.

AFTERTHOUGHTS: The onions may also be baked in a 375°F oven for approximately 45 minutes.

No red onions? Then make yellow or white flowers.

SAGE AND ONION PUDDING

Serves six to eight

This is derived from an old Welsh recipe for steamed leek pudding. After fiddling around with the ubiquitous onion, I came up with this richly flavored bread pudding (and several variations). You could, of course, steam it as in the original recipe if you have a nice pudding mold, but it's just fine baked in a soufflé dish or loaf pan. It's so good it makes my toes curl. Try it with roast chicken and a spoonful of pan gravy.

Enough egg bread or rolls or crustless French bread to yield 3 well-packed cups coarse crumbs
6 tablespoons butter
4 cups diced onion
1 garlic clove, minced
1 cup chicken broth, homemade or canned

2 large eggs
½ cup half-and-half
1 teaspoon dried sage leaves
1 teaspoon dried thyme
Dash of nutmeg
Freshly ground black pepper

Tear bread on a large, clean tea towel and spread to dry for several hours. You may speed this process by drying the crumbs on a cookie sheet in a 300°F oven for about 30 minutes, stirring and turning them occasionally.

Melt 4 tablespoons of the butter and add onions. Cook them over lowish heat until lightly colored, adding garlic near the end of the cooking time. When the onions are done, pour in chicken broth, remove pan from heat, and allow to cool.

Beat eggs and cream together in a large mixing bowl. Stir in sage, thyme, nutmeg, and pepper. Add cooled onion mixture and bread crumbs and mix thoroughly. When well blended, press ingredients down firmly with the back of a spoon and allow it to rest 30 minutes to absorb liquid and flavors.

Preheat oven to 350°F.

Thoroughly butter a soufflé dish or loaf pan, or spray with one of those nonstick pan coatings. Spoon mixture firmly into pan. Bang the pan bottom sharply on a hard surface a couple of times to settle ingredients, and finish by pressing and smoothing the top with your fingers. Strew flakes of remaining butter over the surface.

Place the pan on the center rack of the oven and bake for about 45 minutes, or until firm and nicely browned. Do not overbake—remember, this is bread *pudding,* not a bread loaf. Serve hot or at room temperature or cold—they're all divine.

AFTERTHOUGHTS: You may make this a day ahead. Bake it in a loaf pan, chill thoroughly, slice, and sauté it in butter to go along with creamy scrambled eggs and crisp, thick-sliced bacon.

Then again you might layer it with oysters and lashings of dry sherry.

It's no slouch either with ham or pork chops and homemade coarse applesauce.

SPICED ONIONS WITH PISTACHIOS

Serves eight

The amiable onion in a chic new dress. They look appetizing and taste wonderful—what more can you ask of an onion?

4 *large yellow onions (or Mauis,*	1 *teaspoon grated lemon rind*
if available)	⅛ *teaspoon ground cinnamon*
½ *cup beef broth*	*Pinch of ground cloves*
½ *cup dry red wine*	*Salt*
3 *tablespoons butter*	*Freshly ground black pepper*
2 *teaspoons sugar*	¼ *cup crushed pistachios*

Remove skins from onions, cut in half crosswise, and arrange halves cut side up in a baking pan just large enough to hold them comfortably.

Preheat oven to 350°F.

In a saucepan, combine the broth, wine, 1 tablespoon of the butter, sugar, lemon rind, cinnamon, cloves, and salt and pepper to taste. Bring mixture to a boil, then pour over onions, cover dish tightly with foil, and bake 45 minutes, or until onions are tender.

Melt remaining butter in a small saucepan, add pistachios, and sauté lightly until nuts just begin to turn golden.

Remove foil cover from baking dish. Spoon butter and pistachios over onions and continue baking, uncovered, 10 minutes, or until nuts are lightly browned. Serve immediately.

AFTERTHOUGHT: Serve each onion with a dollop of crème fraîche or sour cream.

ONION RINGS IN BEER BATTER

Serves six

Serve these superb onion rings as I sometimes do with a cruet of malt or red wine vinegar and a small bowl of coarse salt to be shaken and sprinkled by each guest to his taste. Hot pepper vinegar is a kick, too. Make a lot!

1½ cups flour
2 teaspoons sugar
1 teaspoon baking powder
1 teaspoon salt

1 can beer, any kind
Vegetable oil for deep-frying
4 large onions

Sift dry ingredients into a bowl and stir in the beer. Batter should be the consistency of heavy cream. Let it stand for 5 to 10 minutes.

Heat oil to 375°F.

Peel onions and cut into 1/2-inch slices. Separate into rings.

Place rings in batter and gently stir them around so that each one is coated with the batter.

Lift several out of the batter at a time with a long kitchen fork, allowing surplus batter to fall back into the bowl.

Fry onions in hot oil and drain on paper towels. Keep warm in a 200°F oven until all the onions are done. Serve immediately.

AFTERTHOUGHT: This batter also works very well as tempura batter for vegetables.

INDONESIAN CRISP ONION FLAKES
(Goreng Dawang)

About 1 cup

Warning! These are highly addictive! You will find they are a perfect garnish for many, many dishes: omelets, open-face Danish sandwiches, baked potatoes, broiled or steamed fish, fresh noodles, and lots, lots more.

2 medium white onions, peeled   *2 cups peanut oil*

Cut onions in half lengthwise; lay halves cut side down on a cutting board and slice them as thin as possible, or use the slicing disk on a food processor.

Place onions in a single layer on several thicknesses of paper towels. Let stand, uncovered, 1 to 2 hours.

Heat oil in a wok, deep fry pan, or electric skillet over medium heat. Add the onions and fry until the edges begin to turn golden; reduce heat and fry until evenly brown. Remove them with a slotted spoon and drain on paper towels. Allow to stand until cool and dry, and store in an airtight container, or eat them all up.

AFTERTHOUGHT: Try sprinkling them over a finished Tian (page 128 or 196). Or mashed potatoes, or salad. It's endless.

GREEN BEANS LYONNAISE

Serves four

An elegant presentation in the manner of Lyon.

1 pound slender green beans   *Freshly ground black pepper*
1 medium onion, chopped   *Few drops of wine vinegar*
3 tablespoons butter   *Chopped parsley*
Salt

Snap the ends off the beans and leave them whole. Blanch them in a large pot of boiling water for 2 to 4 minutes, or until they are just crisp-tender. Refresh them under cold running water; drain. Pat them dry with paper towels and set aside.

Sauté the chopped onion in 2 tablespoons of the butter until golden and soft. Season with salt and pepper.

Add the beans and another tablespoon of butter to the onions and sauté until the beans begin to brown a little. Add a few drops of wine vinegar, garnish with parsley, and serve at once.

JANSSON'S TEMPTATION

Serves four

Jansson isn't the only one tempted by this happy marriage of onions and potatoes. I love it, and I know you will, too.

6 medium white rose potatoes,
   peeled and sliced thin
Freshly ground black pepper
2 medium onions, minced
16 anchovy fillets, rinsed and
   patted dry

¼ cup dry bread crumbs
1½ cups heavy cream
2 tablespoons butter

Preheat oven to 375°F.

Place a layer of potatoes in a well-buttered gratin dish and season lightly with pepper. Cover with a thin layer of onions and anchovies. Continue layering with the remaining potatoes, onions, and anchovies, lightly seasoning the layers with freshly ground pepper.

Sprinkle the top with crumbs, pour in the cream, and dot with butter.

Bake until the potatoes are tender when tested with a knife. Serve very hot from the dish.

GRATIN OF POTATOES AND ONIONS

Serves four

The perfect marriage.

1 garlic clove, cut in half,
  unpeeled
Butter for gratin dish
3 medium Idaho potatoes,
  scrubbed
2 large or 3 medium onions

Salt
Freshly ground black pepper
1 can beef broth
2 tablespoons butter
1 tablespoon freshly grated
  Parmesan or Romano cheese

Preheat the oven to 400°F.

Rub the bottom and sides of an oval gratin dish with the cut garlic and butter the pan well.

Slice the potatoes, unpeeled (a food processor makes short work of this task). Place them in a bowl of cold water to cover to prevent them from darkening.

Halve the onions from stem to stern and slice them thin. Drain the potatoes and pat dry. Arrange the potatoes and sliced onions in layers in the prepared casserole. Add salt and pepper as you go along. Easy on the salt; the broth may have enough.

Pour enough broth into the dish to cover the vegetables. Dot the top with butter, cover with foil, and bake in the preheated oven until the broth is almost absorbed and the potatoes are tender. Remove the foil, sprinkle with cheese, and increase the heat. When the cheese is golden the potatoes are ready.

TIAN OF EGGPLANT, ZUCCHINI, AND RED ONIONS

Serves four to six

What an exciting way to present the pretty summer vegetables— crisp tender slices composed in a dish alive with bright fresh colors, fragrant herbs, and glistening, fruity olive oil.

3 ripe tomatoes
3 long purple Japanese eggplants
3 large zucchini
2 small red onions, peeled
4–5 sprigs fresh rosemary

4 garlic cloves, minced
½ cup olive oil
Salt
Freshly ground black pepper

Preheat oven to 400°F.

Slice tomatoes 1/2 inch thick. Thinly slice eggplants, zucchini, and onions. Arrange vegetables in a shallow baking dish, alternating the slices. Place rosemary sprigs here and there.

Combine garlic and olive oil and pour over vegetables. Sprinkle with salt and pepper.

Bake in the preheated oven for 30 minutes, or until vegetables are tender. Pour off excess oil if desired, and serve immediately.

SALADS AND DRESSINGS

ONION SALAD WITH CURRY YOGURT DRESSING

Serves four

A delicious salad; fresh and lively.

2 medium oranges
1 teaspoon grated orange peel
1 cup thinly sliced red onions
Spinach leaves

Curry Yogurt Dressing (recipe
* follows)*
2 tablespoons toasted sesame seeds

Grate the oranges before peeling, reserving 2 teaspoons of peel (1 for garnish, 1 for the dressing). Peel and section the oranges, saving any juice.

Separate the onion slices into rings.

Arrange the spinach leaves on serving plates. Top with orange sections and onion rings. Drizzle with dressing and garnish with toasted sesame seeds and a light sprinkling of grated orange peel.

CURRY YOGURT DRESSING

1¼ cups

1 cup plain yogurt
2 tablespoons orange juice
1 tablespoon lemon juice

1 tablespoon mild honey
½ teaspoon curry powder
1 teaspoon grated orange peel

Combine all ingredients, blending well. Taste and ajust seasonings. Store in a covered container in the refrigerator.

FARMER'S SALAD WITH SOUR CREAM DRESSING

Serves four

A good picnic salad; great with cold cuts.

1 medium yellow onion, thinly
  sliced
10 radishes, thinly sliced
½ cucumber, peeled and thinly
  sliced

Sour Cream Dressing (recipe
  follows)
Chopped fresh parsley

Separate the onion slices into rings.

In a serving bowl, combine the onion, radish, and cucumber slices. Dress with sour cream dressing and garnish with parsley.

SOUR CREAM DRESSING

About 1¼ cups

1 cup sour cream
1 teaspoon sugar
4–5 pimiento-stuffed olives,
  coarsely chopped

2 tablespoons chili sauce
2 teaspoons chopped scallions
Salt to taste

Combine ingredients until well blended. Store in a covered container in the refrigerator.

BAVARIAN ONION SALAD WITH SWEET AND SOUR DRESSING

Serves four

Tart, fragrant, crunchy, and a beautiful color.

1 can (16 ounces) julienne beets
Sweet and Sour Dressing (recipe follows)
1 medium red onion, thinly sliced

2 medium Red Delicious apples
Lemon juice
Crisp lettuce

Drain beets thoroughly and marinate in 1/4 cup of the dressing for at least 1 hour.

Separate onion slices into rings and place in a bowl. Cover with boiling water and allow to stand for 3 to 4 minutes. Drain thoroughly and drizzle with dressing. Toss and set aside.

Near serving time, core and slice apples into thin wedges. Sprinkle with lemon juice to prevent browning, and toss gently. Set aside.

Arrange lettuce on individual serving plates.

Lightly toss apples, onions, and beets together. Mound each serving in the centers of lettuce leaves and drizzle with more dressing.

SWEET AND SOUR DRESSING

About 1 cup

3 tablespoons sugar
1 teaspoon Dijon mustard
½ teaspoon salt

1 teaspoon caraway seeds
3 tablespoons white wine vinegar
½ cup salad oil

Combine sugar, mustard, salt, caraway, and vinegar in a blender.

With the motor running, add oil in a thin stream. When all oil is incorporated, shut off motor, taste for seasonings, and correct as necessary. Transfer mixture to a covered container and refrigerate until ready to use.

PORTUGUESE SALAD

Serves four

Fresh and crisp.

1 large green pepper
2 large sweet red peppers
2 small red onions, sliced very
  thin
4 medium tomatoes, peeled,
  seeded, and cut into eighths

Mustard Vinaigrette (page 52)
6 parsley sprigs
6 fresh oregano leaves

Roast the peppers on a rack in a preheated broiler about 6 inches from the flame for approximately 10 minutes, turning them frequently, until their skins are blistered and charred. Place them in a paper bag, close tightly, and allow them to steam until cool enough to handle. Peel them, cut in half lengthwise, remove stem and seeds, and slice them into julienne strips.

Toss the peppers with the onions, tomatoes, and enough vinaigrette to thoroughly moisten, but not drown, the vegetables. Garnish with the parsley and oregano leaves and serve at room temperature.

AFTERTHOUGHT: This becomes Greek with the addition of feta cheese and ripe olives.

ONION SALAD, SWEET AND SOUR
BACON DRESSING

Serves six

This colorful, richly flavored salad is best served warm and is perfect with grilled sausages and dark bread.

8 strips bacon

½ cup red sherry or wine
  vinegar

1 teaspoon Worchestershire sauce

1 teaspoon sugar (or more to
  taste)

Freshly ground black pepper

1 teaspoon dried dillweed
  or
1 tablespoon snippets of fresh dill

¼ cup salad oil

4 medium brown or red onions,
  halved lengthwise and cut into
  eighths

¼ cup minced fresh parsley

Salt

1 bunch watercress, stems
  removed
  or
6 small red cabbage leaves

Sauté the bacon until crisp and drain on paper towels. Crumble and
set aside. Pour off all but 2 tablespoons of the bacon fat.

In the same skillet, combine the vinegar, Worcestershire sauce,
sugar, pepper, dill, and oil and heat gently until the sugar dissolves.
Remove from heat.

Place the cut onions in a big bowl and cover them with boiling
water. Allow to stand for 5 minutes. Drain well and place them in
a serving bowl.

Heat the dressing to a boil and pour it over the onions. Add the
crumbled bacon and parsley and toss. Taste for salt.

At this point you have a choice: you may toss in the watercress
and present the salad in the serving bowl, or you may arrange each
serving on a pretty leaf of red cabbage. Whatever you fancy, remember—serve it warm.

TARRAGON ONION SALAD

Serves six

A nice complement to summer grills.

1½ pounds fresh string beans,
  ends pared

¾ cup good olive oil

¼ cup tarragon vinegar

1 teaspoon fresh tarragon leaves

Salt

Freshly ground pepper

2 garlic cloves, crushed

1½ cups red onions, thinly sliced
  and separated into rings

2 cups grated Gruyère cheese

In a large saucepan, steam beans, covered, until just tender, 6 to 8 minutes.

While beans are still hot, marinate them in a mixture of olive oil, vinegar, tarragon leaves, salt and pepper to taste, and garlic. Allow to remain at room temperature until the beans are cool. Add onion rings, toss well, cover, and refrigerate for at least 3 hours.

Before serving, remove garlic and taste for seasonings and adjust. Add Gruyère and toss again. Serve on lettuce leaves.

RED ONION AND ORANGE SALAD

Serves six

A piquant salad that goes well with roast pork or chops.

3 large navel oranges
2 medium red onions, sliced thin
and separated into rings
2 tablespoons orange juice
1 teaspoon lemon juice (or more
to taste)
1 small garlic clove, minced

1 tablespoon chopped fresh
rosemary
Salt
½ cup light fruity olive oil
2 bunches watercress, washed,
dried, and stems removed

Peel oranges, removing all the white pith while you're at it. Slice them crosswise with a serrated knife and arrange the slices on a large plate. Chill, covered, for at least 15 minutes, or up to several hours.

Soak the onion rings in ice water for at least 30 minutes. Drain thoroughly.

Place the orange and lemon juice, garlic, rosemary, and salt to taste in a blender. With the motor running, add the oil in a thin stream; whirl until the dressing emulsifies.

Arrange the orange slices alternately with the onion rings on a wide, shallow platter. Form a wreath of watercress around the oranges and onions. Just before serving, drizzle the salad with the dressing.

SAUCES

ONION HORSERADISH SAUCE

About 2½ cups

When you bring a doggie bag home, run up a little of this sauce, and forget Fido!

½ cup sour cream
½ cup heavy cream
1 tablespoon horseradish
½ cup minced yellow onion
2 tablespoons capers, chopped

¼ cup chopped chives, plus more
*   for garnish*
Salt
Freshly ground black pepper

Combine sour cream, heavy cream, horseradish, onions, capers, and chives. Add salt and pepper to taste.

Chill until ready to serve. Garnish with a sprinkling of chopped chives.

RED ONION MARMALADE

About 2 cups

The sliced onions give of their essence after a
brew and become ambrosia for gods and men.
—Jane Bothwell

8 tablespoons butter
1½ pounds red onions, sliced
*   very thin*
4 shallots, sliced very thin
½ cup sugar

Salt
Freshly ground black pepper
⅔ cup dry red wine
⅓ cup sherry wine vinegar
3½ tablespoons grenadine

In a large stainless steel or enameled saucepan, melt the butter over moderately low heat. Add the onions, shallots, sugar, and salt and pepper to taste, and combine. Cover and cook slowly, stirring occasionally, for 30 minutes.

Add the wine, vinegar, and grenadine. Bring the mixture to a boil, then cook, uncovered, over moderately low heat for another 30 minutes. Stir occasionally.

At the end of the cooking time, raise the heat to medium and cook, stirring constantly, until mixture is thick. Remove from heat and allow to cool a few minutes.

Transfer the marmalade to a serving bowl and serve warm or cold.

TOMATO, WINE, AND ONION SAUCE

About 4 cups

Devastating with hot or cold pasta.

3 tablespoons olive oil
3 large onions, finely chopped
2 cups good dry red wine (don't use it if you wouldn't drink it)
1 cup water
4 medium-size ripe tomatoes, peeled, seeded, and chopped
6–8 garlic cloves, mashed
2 teaspoons dried thyme
2 teaspoons dried oregano
2 large bay leaves
Salt
Freshly ground black pepper
½ cup oil-cured black olives, pitted
1 tablespoon chopped capers
¼ cup chopped parsley
3 tablespoons chopped gherkins

Heat oil in a heavy skillet. Add onions and cook over low heat until tender, but not colored, about 20 minutes. Add wine and water and bring to a boil. Cook over high heat 5 minutes.

Add tomatoes, garlic, thyme, oregano, bay leaves, salt and pepper to taste, and reduce heat to low. Simmer for 1 hour, stirring occasionally, or until sauce becomes thick.

Remove from heat and cool slightly. Discard bay leaves. Process in a blender or food processor until smooth. Return sauce to the skillet and add remaining ingredients. Cook over medium heat another 5 minutes. Taste for seasonings and adjust as necessary.

AFTERTHOUGHT: Poach eggs in this sauce for a real treat.

SAUCE SOUBISE

About 2½ cups

This sauce is a bit bland for my taste, but it is a classic onion recipe, so here it is.

½ pound white onions
2 tablespoons butter
¼ cup flour
2 cups rich milk or chicken broth

Salt
Freshly ground black pepper
Pinch of nutmeg
Dash of cayenne

Peel the onions and slice them thin. Cook them gently in the butter in a small saucepan for 10 to 15 minutes. Stir in the flour and cook 2 to 3 minutes.

Gradually add the milk or broth, stirring as it thickens. Season with salt, pepper, nutmeg, and cayenne and simmer over low heat for 15 to 20 minutes. Watch it—don't let it scorch. Remove from heat and allow to cool a few minutes.

Taste for seasoning and purée in the blender. Reheat slowly and serve this sauce hot with roast lamb.

BAVARIAN MELTED ONION SAUCE

3½ cups

This is especially good with grilled calf's liver.

6 slices bacon, diced
6 medium onions, minced
3 cups beef broth

⅓ cup minced fresh parsley
Lemon juice
Freshly ground black pepper

In a large heavy skillet, cook the bacon over medium-low heat, stirring until lightly brown. Discard most of the fat, leaving about 2 tablespoons.

Add the onions and sauté over moderate heat for 15 minutes, or until they are translucent.

Add the beef broth and bring to a boil. Reduce heat and simmer for 30 minutes.

Add parsley and season with a squeeze of lemon juice and a grinding of black pepper.

ONION, CHILI, AND CHEESE SAUCE

About 2 cups

This zingy little sauce is so good served in crisp baked potato skins for a first course. It's equally delicious as a topping for freshly baked potatoes. And try it served with Garlic Pita Toasts (page 64) and black olives.

5 large fresh poblano or
  Anaheim chilies
1 large onion, halved lengthwise
  and cut into ¼-inch strips
2 tablespoons butter
1 cup heavy cream

2 ounces Monterey jack cheese,
  grated
2 ounces Cheddar cheese, grated
4–5 leaves fresh cilantro
Pinch of toasted, crushed cumin
  seeds

Roast the peppers in the broiler about 6 inches from the flame until their skins have blistered and charred, turning them often. Remove them from the broiler and place them immediately into a brown paper bag, twisting it closed. Let them steam until cool enough to handle, then peel off their skins. Cut them in half lengthwise, remove stems and seeds, and slice them into strips about 4 inches long and 1/4 inch thick. Set aside.

In a skillet sauté the onions slowly in butter, stirring occasionally until soft. Add the chilies and cook for 1 minute longer.

Add the cream and simmer for 8 minutes, or until it is thickened. Remove from the heat and stir in the cheeses.

Before serving, garnish with cilantro leaves and cumin seeds.

SAUCE TI-MALICE

About 1 cup

Serve this Haitian sauce with roast or barbecued pork and sautéed bananas and yams. It's a touch of culinary voodoo.

1½ cups finely chopped onions
¾ cup lime juice
2 tablespoons butter
2 teaspoons finely chopped fresh
  hot chilies

1 teaspoon finely minced garlic
2 teaspoons salt
½ teaspoon sugar

Mix onions and lime juice and marinate 1 hour at room temperature. Drain onions through a sieve. Reserve marinade.

Melt butter over moderate heat in a heavy saucepan. Add onions and sauté 5 minutes, until soft and transparent. Do not brown. Adjust heat as necessary.

Add chopped chilies and garlic, lower heat, and simmer, covered, about 10 minutes. Remove from heat and stir in reserved marinade, salt, and sugar. Cool.

AFTERTHOUGHT: Store, refrigerated, for about 5 days in a covered container.

ONION CHUTNEY

About 1 cup

Serve this spicy chutney warm or cold with grilled meats or chicken.

⅔ cup thinly sliced yellow onions
2 tablespoons light olive oil
½ cup water
1 teaspoon mild honey
3 dried apricot halves, chopped
½ cup golden raisins

1 tablespoon chopped pickled
  jalapeño peppers (or to taste)
1 teaspoon balsamic vinegar
Salt
4–5 fresh cilantro leaves

Sauté the onion slices in the olive oil until soft. Add the water, honey, and apricots, and cook over high heat for 5 minutes, stirring frequently, until most of the liquid is absorbed and the mixture is thickened.

Stir in the raisins, jalapeños, balsamic vinegar, and salt, and cook over low heat, covered, for 5 minutes, or until the raisins are plump.

Serve hot or cold, garnished with cilantro leaves.

ONION SORBET

About 1 quart

This is wonderful with cold meats. Serve the sorbet in pretty lettuce cups, avocado halves, small green pepper halves, or hollowed-out small (not cherry—they're too small) tomatoes.

⅔ cup sugar
⅔ cup water
3 large yellow onions, boiled, drained, and puréed
¼ cup wine vinegar
¼ cup finely minced fresh parsley

2 scallions, finely minced (including 3 inches of green top)
½ teaspoon salt
1 cup plain yogurt
Minced fresh parsley and/or chives

Combine the sugar and water in a small saucepan. Over medium-high heat, cook and stir until sugar is dissolved. Just before the boil, remove syrup from heat and allow to cool. Cover and refrigerate.

Combine onion purée, vinegar, parsley, scallions, salt, and chilled syrup and blend well. Place mixture in an ice cream maker and freeze until sorbet is still soft. Add yogurt and continue churning. (If using a conventional freezer, freeze in a stainless-steel container. Thaw partially, spoon mixture into a food processor or blender, and process until smooth. Add yogurt and blend well. Refreeze.)

Serve garnished with parsley and/or chives.

BREADS

GOUGÈRE

12 large puffs

Gougère is the deservedly famous hot cheese pastry the Burgundians serve with their glorious wines. Though traditionally baked in a wreathlike ring, here they are presented in individual puffs. Gougère also lends itself to tiny cocktail puffs, filled with savory mixtures like Garlic Tapenade (page 9), salmon mousse, or pâté.

1 cup water
8 tablespoons butter
1 teaspoon salt
1 cup all-purpose flour
4 eggs, at room temperature
1 small onion, diced and sautéed
*   until tender in 1 tablespoon*
*   butter*

1 cup cubed Gruyère cheese or
*   half Parmesan, half Gruyère*
Additional cheese, grated, for
*   topping (optional)*

Combine water, butter, and salt in a medium saucepan and bring to a boil. Reduce heat to medium and add flour, stirring vigorously until batter has thickened and forms a shiny ball.

Add eggs, one at a time, completely incorporating each egg before adding the next. (An electric hand mixer works just fine here.) Stir in onion and cheese.

Preheat oven to 375°F.

Drop the batter by egg-size lumps onto an ungreased cookie sheet, spacing the dough about 2 inches apart. Drop them lightly, keeping the batter high so it will not spread out too far during baking. Top each puff with a bit of grated cheese, if you wish.

Bake on the center rack of the preheated oven for 15 to 20 minutes, or until the gougères are puffed and well browned. When they are done, turn off the oven, remove them, and pierce the side of each puff with a sharp knife. Return them to the turned-off oven and let them rest there, with the door open, to dry and crisp a few minutes (otherwise they will steam and fall). Serve hot.

SPEEDY RAISED ONION BISCUITS

10 to 12 biscuits

You can run up these jazzy biscuits in a flash, and they couldn't be any better if you fiddled around for hours in the kitchen. The yeast raises them to new heights and smells wonderful to boot. I like to give them a few grindings of pepper before baking.

1 package active dry yeast	*1 medium onion, shredded fine*
1 teaspoon sugar	*1 tablespoon butter*
2 tablespoons warm water	*4 tablespoons melted butter*
2 cups biscuit mix	*1 tablespoon poppy seeds*
1 cup milk	

Combine yeast, sugar, and warm water in a small bowl and let stand until foamy.

Place biscuit mix and milk in another bowl and stir well to blend. Add yeast mixture and combine.

Turn out on a lightly floured board and knead for a few seconds. Form into a smooth ball, cover, and let it rest while you prepare the onions.

Melt 1 tablespoon butter in a small skillet and when it is foamy add shredded onion. Sauté until clear and beginning to brown. When pale brown, remove from the fire. Watch carefully so that it doesn't burn. Place the onions on a plate to cool faster.

Roll the dough out into a rectangle about 8 × 15 inches, and brush with half the melted butter. Spread the cooled onions evenly over half the dough, and sprinkle with poppy seeds. Fold remaining half over onions and press the edges together. Brush the top with melted butter and cut into rounds. Place biscuits in a buttered baking tin with their edges barely touching. Cover and allow to rise for about 40 minutes.

Preheat the oven to 400°F. Bake the biscuits for about 20 minutes, or until golden brown.

AFTERTHOUGHT: How about these onion beauties with creamed leeks?

Slice 4 medium to large leeks (white part only). Cook in 2 tablespoons butter until wilted. Add a cup of chicken broth and boil liquid down by half. Add a cup of cream, some salt and pepper, and reduce until thick and perfect. Add a dash of cayenne and a few drops of lemon juice and keep warm. Spoon the creamed leeks over split biscuits. Serve with several slices of Canadian bacon, some fresh orange juice, and stand back!

GOLDEN ONION LOAF CAKE

Serves six to eight

This glory is from the redoubtable Bert Greene. If you're at all concerned about your figure, turn the page quickly.

Beer Batter (recipe follows)	*1¼ cups grated Monterey jack*
2 large Bermuda onions (about	*cheese, regular or jalapeño*
2 pounds)	*Salt*
Vegetable oil for frying	*Freshly ground black pepper*

Make the Beer Batter.

Cut the onions into 1/4-inch-thick slices. Place the sliced onions in a large bowl, cover with ice water, and let stand 30 minutes.

Heat 2 inches of oil in a large heavy saucepan until hot but not smoking. Drain the onions, divide into rings, and lightly pat them dry.

Dip the onions into the batter, shaking off any excess. Fry them in the hot oil, about four or five at a time, until golden brown. Drain on paper towels.

Preheat the oven to 400°F. Generously butter an 8-inch or 9-inch springform pan. Line the sides with onion rings. Place one third of the remaining onion rings over the bottom. Sprinkle with 1/2 cup of the grated cheese. Add another layer of onion rings and sprinkle with 1/2 cup of the cheese. Top with the remaining onion rings and sprinkle with the remaining 1/4 cup of cheese. Bake 15 minutes.

To remove the springform pan, first run a knife around the edges. Remove the sides of the pan, then gently flip the onion loaf over onto a serving platter. Carefully remove the bottom of the pan. Sprinkle with salt and pepper to taste.

BEER BATTER

About 3 1/2 cups

1 cup all-purpose flour
2 teaspoons dry mustard
1 teaspoon freshly grated nutmeg
½ teaspoon salt

4 eggs, separated
2 teaspoons Dijon mustard
1 cup beer

Combine the flour with the dry mustard, nutmeg, and salt in a medium bowl.

Combine the egg yolks with the Dijon mustard and beer. Add this to the flour mixture and stir until smooth. Refrigerate, covered, 8 hours.

Just before using the batter, beat the egg whites until stiff; fold them into the batter.

ZWIEBELKUCHEN

Two 12-inch flat breads

Serve this hearty German onion bread hot with ice cold beer or white wine.

1 package active dry yeast
1 cup warm water
1 tablespoon brown sugar
4 tablespoons vegetable oil
1 teaspoon salt
1 egg
2 cups all-purpose flour
2 cups rye flour

2 tablespoons butter
7 large brown onions, sliced thin
  and separated into rings
¾ cup finely chopped ham
½ teaspoon caraway seeds
  (optional)
Freshly ground black pepper

Combine yeast and water and allow to rest 5 minutes. Combine sugar, 3 tablespoons of the oil, salt, egg, and all-purpose flour in a food processor or electric mixer and blend 5 minutes. Add the yeast mixture.

Place flour mixture in a large bowl and gradually beat in enough rye flour to form a soft dough, about 2 cups. Knead on a floured board 8 to 10 minutes, or until smooth. Place in a greased bowl, cover with a tea towel, and let rise in a warm place until dough has nearly doubled, about 1 hour.

While dough is rising, heat butter and remaining tablespoon of oil in a large skillet. Add onions and sauté over medium-low heat until they are soft and golden, about 45 minutes. Don't rush this step, as slow cooking will mellow and sweeten them. Stir in the ham and caraway seeds. Taste for seasonings and adjust as necessary.

Preheat oven to 450°F.

Punch down dough and divide in half. Pat and stretch each half over the bottom of two well-greased 12-inch pizza pans. Spread each with the onion mixture and a few grindings of black pepper.

Bake in preheated oven for 15 to 20 minutes, or until crusts are nicely browned. Cut in wedges and serve immediately.

ONION BREAD

One loaf

This basic recipe is a cinch to make, and once you get the hang of it, you'll get a kick out of serving your own crusty bread. When the dough is shaped into a long slender loaf and filled with onions, it's a fine thing to serve just as it comes from the oven. On the other hand, the very same long loaf is a great base for a batch of Provençal sandwiches or heros. Then again, you may choose to shape the dough into rolls of a generous size, perfect for grilled hamburgers. Or, roll the dough out into a circle about 1 inch thick and, instead of mixing the onions into the dough, spread them over the top, sprinkle them lavishly with good olive oil, and you have a flaky *focaccia*.

One of my favorite ways to serve this loaf is to skip the onions and add 1/2 cup seeded muscat raisins and 3 tablespoons chopped fresh rosemary to the dough. After the first rising, bake the shaped loaf in a springform pan. This one is a real crowd pleaser. Or add a quarter pound of prosciutto (in big shreds) and sauté it along with the onions. That's a winner.

Red onions are the best to use in this recipe; they give it a tangy sweetness.

1 package active dry yeast	*1 garlic clove, minced*
¼ teaspoon sugar	*Cornmeal for the baking pan*
1⅔ cups water	
3½ cups all-purpose flour	GLAZE
2 teaspoons salt	*2 teaspoons water*
4 tablespoons olive oil	*1 egg yolk*
1 large red onion, chopped fine	*1 teaspoon poppy seeds (optional)*

Place the yeast, sugar, and 1/3 cup of the water in a small bowl. Allow the mixture to stand until it is bubbly, about 10 minutes.

Place the yeast mixture, 3 cups of the flour, and the salt in a food processor. Add the remaining water and 2 tablespoons of the olive oil. Process until you have a nice smooth dough, turning the machine off and on as it mixes.

Sprinkle the remaining 1/2 cup flour onto your kneading surface and knead the dough; slap it around, adding more flour if necessary. (If you are not using a food processor, knead for about 10 minutes.) When the dough is satiny and not sticky, place it in a lightly oiled bowl, cover, and allow it to stand in a warm place until it triples, 2 to 2 1/2 hours.

Meanwhile, heat the remaining 2 tablespoons of oil in a skillet and sauté the onion and garlic for about 3 minutes. Set aside.

When the dough has risen, turn it out onto a floured surface, punch it down, and roll it out into a circle about 1/2 inch thick. Spread the onion mixture over the dough. Fold the left third over the center; cover with the right third. Fold the top third over the center; cover with the bottom third. Turn the dough over and place it in an oiled bowl. Cover and allow it to rise 1 hour.

Punch the dough down, turn it out on a floured board, and allow it to rest for 3 minutes. Knead briefly and repeat the folding steps above. Form the dough into a long loaf and place it on a baking sheet sprinkled with cornmeal. Cover and allow it to rise until doubled, about 1 hour.

Preheat the oven to 400°F. Place a roasting pan half-filled with water in the bottom of the oven. Make 3 slashes across the top of the loaf with a very sharp knife or razor blade. Combine the 2 teaspoons of water with the egg yolk; brush this over the top of the loaf. Sprinkle with poppy seeds.

Place the bread on its baking sheet on the top third of the oven. Bake 30 minutes. Remove the pan of water; continue to bake for an additional 25 minutes.

AFTERTHOUGHT: With a spray bottle, spritz the baking pan before placing on the loaf. Do not use cornmeal. Bake the bread on the top third of the oven for 50 to 55 minutes, misting the loaf occasionally as it browns.

3 The
Gilded Lilies

Gilded . . . ornamentation to something beautiful in its own right.
                    —*Webster's Dictionary*

*T*he rest of the spirited family—down home and earthy, high-powered, elegant and sophisticated, delicate—they run the gamut.

The Diplomatic Leek

Often referred to as the "asparagus of the poor," leeks have been cherished all over Europe for centuries. The emperor Nero was one of their earliest fans. He drank a potion of leeks daily, convinced that it improved his singing voice. Too bad it didn't improve his relationships with his wives (and possibly his political stance, as well), but that's asking a lot of a vegetable, even the mighty leek.

The formidable Charlemagne favored leeks greatly; by his royal edict they were planted all over France, where they flourish today.

Leeks were valued so highly by the Welsh that they chose them for their national emblem, and wore them, polished and gleaming, in their hatbands when they rode into battle.

No wonder. The leek is a handsome plant, tall and sturdy. Its pearly base is shaded from palest green to rich, deep green leaves that crown the stalk with a series of overlapping chevrons—a flawless design. The subtle flavor and silken texture is unmatched by any member of the peerless lily family.

Until lately, leeks have been given short shrift in our own country; regarded as an exotic rarity, scarce and horrifyingly expensive, with a bunch of complicated, threatening directions for cleaning. The truth is that leeks are not all that hard to clean; a little boring, perhaps, but altogether too much has been made of what is really a very simple matter.

As for availability, leeks are beginning to appear more widely in supermarkets and greengrocers all year. (If you live anywhere near a farmers' market, the kind of weekly market held in many cities, you're in luck, for that's the place to find nice fresh leeks at very favorable prices.) As our cooking becomes more sophisticated and we learn to use the noble leek in all its delicious ways, our best shot is to keep asking for them at the market, and figure that the reliable old law of supply and demand will come through for us. Keep demanding!

Leeks may look like great big scallions, but the resemblence ends there, for they have a delicate taste and texture, while the rowdy scallions retain their lusty charm, raw or cooked. Refined and amiable, the leek is the aristocrat of the lily family and mingles easily with many other foods. It brings a subtle character and depth to delicate creamy soups and elegant sauces, and marries well with the more robust dishes of meat, fish, and poultry. Leeks may be braised, sautéed, stir-fried, grilled, blanched, or marinated; they make fine tarts, omelets, and distinctive soups, and the mellow flavor of young leeks shows off admirably in culinary riffs composed of leeks alone, cold or hot, with the simplest of sauces or dressings.

Leeks range in size from the slender stalks of spring, not much larger than scallions, to the kingly specimens up to three inches in diameter. The large, mature leeks often have a thickening flower stalk developing in their centers that will have to be discarded. Elderly leeks may also have a coarser flavor and texture, and are best reserved for the soup pot or as an embellishment for stock, where they are justly famous as "the king of soup onions."

For most purposes I prefer leeks one to one and a half inches in diameter, though a special place is reserved, at least by me, for the tender young leeks of summer, braised in a light red wine with a bit of butter and salt and pepper, nothing more.

Whether chopped or minced, sliced into circles, julienne, or diagonals, or left whole, leeks *must* be slightly undercooked—over-cooked leeks lose their lovely color, their texture, and fall apart madly. Keep this in mind especially when blanching them. When they are just barely tender, drain and refresh them in cold water before proceeding.

Leeks are usually sold in bunches of two to six, and weigh about a pound altogether. When you buy them, look for the ones that are of medium size with bright, fresh green tops, the white stalk smooth and unblemished. Store them in the refrigerator unwashed with roots attached, wrapped loosely in plastic, for up to two weeks with no loss of quality. After that, it's all downhill.

Now, for the matter of cleaning. Cut off roots and trim off all but about two inches of green top (about where the light green begins to darken). If you wish, freeze the tops for flavoring soups. Discard any shabby outer leaves. With a sharp knife, slice them through lengthwise to within one inch of the base. Fan out the leaves and run them under cool water to dislodge any grit and dirt. If you are planning to use them whole, cut down one side only. When you are sure they are clean, drain thoroughly. Simple.

Two pounds of leeks become 1 pound cleaned, which is approximately 4 cups chopped, and 2 cups cooked.

One last word: please cook leeks *slowly, gently.* They don't respond well to harsh cooking.

Shallots: The Queen of the Lilies

Shallots—how I love them. Undeniably expensive and elusive, they were sought after by the earliest Roman epicures, and are the chosen favorites of artists of French haute cuisine today.

The regal sauces: beurre rouge, beurre blanc, hollandaise, and marchand du vin? Not without the queenly shallot!

Their smooth violet skins hold a mélange of flavor, a hint of sweetness. Slightly nutty with a touch of onion; crisp and fresh, they are never hot. Always suave and refined, shallots are the grace notes, the crowning touch of fine cooking. A rich dowry indeed.

They are found in three colors—red, greenish white, and lavender, which is the best. Look for shallots that are firm and full, with no sprouts or bruises. If withered or dried out, pass them by, for so is their flavor.

Store them like onions, in an airy, cool spot. If you don't use them heavily, as I do, buy them in small quantities.

One plump shallot yields approximately 1 tablespoon chopped.

Remember that shallots cook quickly, but that doesn't mean they like high heat. Give them the gentle handling they deserve and receive their lovely flavor and delicate color with pleasure.

Scallions

Sassy and bodacious, scallions share with all the culinary lillies numberless inventive presentations, alone or in concert with other members of the allium family.

Like the trusty brown onions, scallions are always around, and may often be substituted for the elusive shallots and leeks without making a big deal out of it.

Look for scallions that have bright green tops and firm white bulbs; avoid the limp ones. Store them, unwashed, in a plastic bag in the refrigerator.

When you are ready to use them, trim off roots and raggedy tops, and remove any unattractive outer leaves. Rinse them under cold running water, drain, pat them dry with paper towels, and there you are—scallions ready to please.

Chives: The Dancers

Pretty chives, their dainty hollow stalks filled with a merry pepperiness and a delicate oniony flavor.

A thankful plant that is simple to grow, it thrives in a pot. Give them a sunny place to live and a little water, and they'll give you their all. They are also happy in the garden, where they multiply enthusiastically and even make fluffy lavender flowers for pretty garnishes.

Largely undervalued, they merit a much wider acclaim for they are much, much more than a casual garnish for baked potatoes. Tarts, omelets, and crêpes are enlived by them; alone, they make an elegant soup. The perfect garnish—the smiling presence to finished dishes.

Choose small bundles of bright green unblemished and unwithered stalks. Keep them in a plastic bag in the refrigerator, where they will stay fresh for about three days.

Snip them with scissors for best results, or use a *very* sharp knife and quick, slicing strokes. Any other method crushes out their juices, alas.

FIRST COURSES

BEGGAR'S PURSES WITH CAVIAR

Serves four

An enchanting first course—delectable chive-scented crêpes filled with caviar and crème fraîche and tied with ribbons of chives. Serve this fantasy with icy vodka or a clear, fresh champagne.

2 eggs at room temperature
½ teaspoon salt
2 teaspoons melted butter
1½ cups milk
1 cup Wondra flour
1 bunch long chives; save 14 for
ribbons; mince the rest

1 small jar Tsar Nicholai
California Golden Caviar
Crème fraîche or sour cream
12 thin lemon slices
¼ cup clarified butter
Watercress sprigs or chive flowers

Whisk eggs, salt, butter, and milk together in a bowl. Add flour, whisking constantly. Fold in minced chives and stir. Let stand 20 minutes.

Dip reserved chives into boiling water until limp, about 10 seconds. Set aside.

Heat a crêpe pan or a small, nonstick skillet over moderate heat. Lightly butter pan. Stir batter and pour about 3 tablespoons (a scant 1/4 cup) into pan, swirling mixture so that it covers the entire bottom. Turn crêpe when edges are slightly dry. Cook on other side about 30 seconds. Remove crêpe to a plate. Proceed with cooking, stirring batter before each addition (or chives remain submerged), until used up. You should end up with 12 or 14 crêpes.

Trim off crisped edges to 6 inches in diameter. Put 1 teaspoon of caviar in the center of each crêpe and a small spoonful of crème fraîche. Gather edges of crêpe together to form a "purse," much like a drawstring bag, and tie a chive ribbon around the gathers near the top. Clip excess ribbon. (Have a friend on hand to share in the tying and fun).

Place 3 thin lemon slices on each serving plate. In a 10-inch skillet, heat clarified butter until hot. Place the purses into butter until just heated. Place 1 purse on each lemon slice, drizzle with butter, and garnish with a watercress sprig or chive flower.

AFTERTHOUGHT: If you cannot find chives, use scallions. Mince an equivalent amount of green for the crêpe batter. Trim ends of scallion leaves and slice into 1/8-inch-long slices for ribbons.

CHINESE ONION PANCAKES

Six 4-inch pancakes

These crisp, flavorful pancakes are delicious when cut into fourths and served with drinks; and they're great with savory Chinese stir-fry dishes. They are fun to make and you may prepare them early in the day if you wish, or even freeze them. Just reheat in a hot oven for a few minutes before serving.

⅔ cup all-purpose flour	*Peanut oil*
¼ cup plus 1 tablespoon	*Salt*
lukewarm water	*3 scallions, chopped*

Mix flour and water and knead until the dough is smooth. Roll into a cylinder 6 inches long and cut into 6 equal pieces. Roll out each piece into a 4-inch round.

With your fingers, coat each round with peanut oil on one side only. Sprinkle with salt and 1 teaspoon of chopped scallions. Roll up like a jelly roll and pull lightly on both ends to stretch. Now coil the roll around in a snakelike fashion, tuck the ends in, and roll out into a 4-inch round. Keep them covered with a damp tea towel while you fry them one at a time.

In a small skillet, heat enough peanut oil to cover the bottom generously. When the oil is hot but not smoking, slip the pancake into the skillet, pressing it flat with a spatula for a few seconds to prevent it from curling. Fry until golden brown. Drain on paper towels.

Cookery means the knowledge of Medea and
of Circe and of Helen and of the Queen of
Sheba.
—John Ruskin

PASTA À LA RUSSE

Serves four as a first course

Mr. Ruskin might well have had this sumptuous dish in mind when
he wrote those words, for it is seductive, simple, and utterly ravish-
ing. While this recipe will serve four, I prefer two, and bring on
the heavy artillery. Chill the bubbly, don your tiara, warm the
porcelain plates, light the candles—and a little night music, please.
The subtle, wily shallot is the perfect undertone.

2 cups heavy cream
1 ounce vodka
3 shallots, minced
Salt
Freshly ground black pepper
8 ounces delicate, fresh pasta (a
must), cooked and hot

Sweet butter
Crème fraîche or sour cream
1 small jar Tsar Nicolai
California Golden Caviar

Place the cream in a small saucepan and simmer it over medium
heat until it thickens slightly. Add the vodka and shallots and continue to simmer for a few more minutes. Remove from heat and
season with a little salt and a grinding of pepper.

Mix the hot pasta with a dollop of sweet butter. Add the cream-
shallot mixture and toss gently. Arrange the pasta in nests on heated
plates and place a generous spoonful of crème fraîche in the center.
Spoon over that as much of the golden caviar as you dare.

Each (or your only) guest may swirl the cream, caviar, and pasta
together. Drink a toast to love, celebrate the moment, and tomor-
row be damned!

SALMON TARTARE WITH SCALLIONS

Serves four

As you know, the salmon is effectively cooked by the lime marinade, and retains all its delicate color and flavor. A light, delicious first course that your guests will thank you for. The salmon and scallions may be prepared well in advance or you can assemble it in a flash for another *coup de cuisine.*

4 ounces fresh raw salmon
Juice of 1 lime or lemon
Salt
Freshly ground black pepper
3–4 bunches slender scallions
   (totaling 20–25 scallions)

1½ cups chicken broth
1 cup Vinaigrette (page 52)
Watercress leaves

Chop the salmon into small dice and combine with lime juice, salt, and pepper to taste. Cover and marinate at least 2 hours in the refrigerator, stirring once or twice.

Meanwhile, wash the scallions and trim them into 6-inch lengths. Bring the chicken broth to a boil, add the scallions, reduce the heat, and simmer until just tender. Do not overcook. Drain them well (save the broth for another use), and coat them with the vinaigrette. Cover and chill for at least 1 1/2 hours.

To serve, arrange the scallions on chilled salad plates, allowing 5 or 6 per serving. Garnish with the marinated salmon, a grinding of pepper, and a leaf or two of watercress.

SCALLOPS AND LEEKS IN CRÈME FRAÎCHE

Serves four

Diplomatic leeks give their essence to this silken, delicate dish.

*1 pound slender leeks (about 8),
    white part only, well washed
    and cut into 2-inch
    matchsticks*
4 tablespoons unsalted butter
*2 tablespoons finely chopped
    shallots*
1 pound bay scallops

¼ cup dry vermouth
½ cup dry white wine
*½ cup crème fraîche or heavy
    cream*
Salt
*½ teaspoon green peppercorns,
    finely chopped*
1 small bunch chives, minced

Place the leeks, 2 tablespoons of the butter, and 1/2 cup cold water in a saucepan; cover and simmer for 20 minutes over low heat. Stir occasionally. When the leeks are tender, remove from heat, set aside, and keep warm.

Heat the remaining 2 tablespoons butter in a saucepan with the shallots. Add the scallops, vermouth, and white wine. Bring the liquid to a boil and immediately reduce the heat; simmer for 2 minutes. Lift out the scallops with a slotted spoon and transfer them to the saucepan holding the leeks, keeping them warm.

Return the wine mixture to high heat along with any juices that may have accumulated from the leeks. Reduce the liquid until about 1/3 cup remains. Add crème fraîche and let it bubble gently for a minute. Stir in a pinch of salt and the green peppercorns. Taste for seasoning.

Pour the hot sauce over the scallops and leeks. Stir gently to coat them with sauce. Serve at once in warmed soup plates. Sprinkle with chives.

AFTERTHOUGHTS: Serve in Pepperidge Farm patty shells, baked according to the directions on the package. Garnish with snipped chives.

If you wish to go all out, ask the fishmonger for scallop shells (scallops come already shucked in the U.S.). You can also buy scallop shells in specialty food shops. Scrub them, rinse, and dry. Pipe the edges with rosettes of whipped potatoes, broil until lightly browned, and spoon in the hot scallops and leeks. Oh my!

MUSSELS, FISHERMAN'S STYLE

Serves four

Just lay in a supply of crusty French bread and plenty of it.

4 pounds mussels (New Zealand, if possible)	Salt
4–5 sizable shallots	Freshly ground black pepper
1 medium onion	⅔ cup heavy cream (optional)
1 teaspoon herbes de Provence	2 tablespoons finely chopped parsley
1½ cups dry white wine or vermouth	

Clean the mussels carefully and remove the beards. Discard any that are not tightly closed.

Peel and chop the shallots and onion and put them in a large pot with the herbs and wine. Boil for 8 to 10 minutes. Add the mussels, cover the pan, and steam them over high heat, turning them occasionally until they have all opened, about 5 minutes. There will usually be one or two reluctant to open; discard them.

Spoon the mussels into four deep soup bowls. Perfectionists will strain the liquid through cheesecloth, but if it doesn't look sandy to you, pour it carefully into another pan, leaving any sand and grit in the bottom of the first pan.

Bring the broth to a boil, check the seasoning, and add salt and pepper to taste. Add the cream here if you are using it. Pour the broth over the mussels, sprinkle with parsley, and give everyone a spoon to eat this delicious stuff.

AFTERTHOUGHT: I like to finish the broth with a couple of spoonfuls of Pernod.

❧

CALIFORNIA CEVICHE

Serves four

I usually serve this light, refreshing concoction in chilled long-stemmed goblets. It looks beautiful, very few calories lurk, and no guilt attaches to one's enjoyment—what a treat! Personally I like a lot of jalapeños, but please yourself.

1 pound bay scallops, or any firm-fleshed white saltwater (not freshwater) fish (or a combination), cut into ½-inch dice
Fresh lime juice to cover fish
Salt
2 pickled jalapeño peppers, seeded and minced

1 small avocado, cut into ½-inch dice
1 small ripe tomato, cored, juiced, and minced
2 or 3 scallions, minced
1 tablespoon torn cilantro leaves
Sprigs of cilantro for garnish

In a deep glass or stainless-steel bowl, combine fish with enough lime juice to barely cover. Cover bowl with plastic wrap and refrigerate 2 hours, stirring fish occasionally.

Add remaining ingredients except cilantro. Chill for another 30 minutes to 1 hour.

Just before serving, taste for seasonings. Add torn cilantro leaves and mix lightly. Serve garnished with sprigs of cilantro.

AFTERTHOUGHTS: For a milder chili flavor, try substituting a small, fresh, seeded, stemmed, and minced Anaheim for the jalapeños.

Try substituting shallots for the scallions for a nice variation.

꽃

SCALLION PARMESAN SOUFFLÉ WITH TOMATO COULIS

Serves four

This delectable soufflé makes a dandy first course, but it requires an attentive audience. Serve with a spoonful of delicate Tomato Coulis.

1 cup finely chopped scallions
4 tablespoons butter
5 tablespoons flour
1½ cups milk
1¼ cups freshly grated
  Parmesan cheese
⅓ cup minced fresh parsley
5 large egg yolks

Pinch of cayenne
Pinch of freshly grated nutmeg
Salt
6 large egg whites, at room
  temperature
Pinch of cream of tartar
Tomato Coulis (recipe follows)

Preheat oven to 400°F.

In a saucepan, cook the scallions in butter over medium heat, stirring occasionally, for 2 minutes. Stir in the flour, and cook, stirring constantly, for 3 minutes. Add the milk and simmer the mixture, stirring frequently, 8 to 10 minutes. Cool mixture for a few minutes.

In a large bowl, combine the cheese, parsley, egg yolks, cayenne, nutmeg, and salt to taste. Pour in the scallion mixture and blend well. Set aside.

Beat the egg whites with the cream of tartar until they just hold stiff peaks. Stir one third of the whites into the yolk mixture, and fold in the remaining whites. Do not overmix.

Spoon the mixture into a well-buttered 1 1/2- to 2-quart soufflé dish. Form a hat by running your thumb around the edge of the soufflé. This will help it rise without spilling over.

Set the soufflé in the center of the preheated oven; reduce heat immediately to 375°F. Bake for 25 to 30 minutes without opening oven door, or until puffed and browned. Keep a close watch. Serve immediately with Tomato Coulis.

TOMATO COULIS

About 1 1/2 cups

A fondue or light sauce, coulis is a simple and tasty accompaniment for soufflés and timbales, poached chicken or fish, or how about soft-scrambled eggs?

6 *ripe tomatoes*
2 *tablespoons minced shallots*
2 *tablespoons butter*
Salt

Freshly ground black pepper
Fresh herbs such as basil,
   parsley, chives

Bring a large saucepan of water to a full boil. Drop in tomatoes and leave them 15 seconds. Remove with a slotted spoon and cool under cold running water. When cool enough to handle, pull off skin with a paring knife. Core, halve, and gently squeeze out seeds and juice. Chop pulp and set aside.

Sauté the minced shallots in butter in a small pan for a minute or two without browning. Add tomato pulp and cook over moderately high heat for several minutes until juices have evaporated and it has thickened to a sauce. Season carefully with salt and pepper to taste. Just before serving, fold in herbs.

AFTERTHOUGHTS: Add a bit of minced garlic with the shallots if desired.

You may like to use scallions instead of shallots, or even finely minced onion.

SOUPS

FRESH TOMATO SOUP

Serves eight to ten

If, as a child, you loved Campbell's tomato soup like I did, wait until you taste this one. We're grown up now and this beautiful soup will change your point of view forever—and you'll be a better person for it. Every minute you spend over a hot stove creating this marvelous potion is well spent; the smiles of contentment are your reward.

⅓ cup light olive oil
4 large onions, sliced
4–5 large shallots, chopped
2 garlic cloves, chopped
2 carrots, peeled and sliced
2 ribs celery, scraped of heavy
    strings and sliced
Parsley sprigs
Salt

Freshly ground black pepper
1 teaspoon sugar
Juice of 1 lemon
4 pounds very ripe red tomatoes,
    peeled
3 tablespoons tomato paste
5 cups beef or chicken broth
Fresh herbs (chives, basil, thyme,
    and/or marjoram), minced

Heat the olive oil in a large, heavy pot and add the onions, shallots, and garlic. Cook, stirring occasionally, until slightly softened, about 5 minutes. Add the carrots, celery, parsley sprigs, salt and pepper to taste, sugar, and lemon juice. Stir to blend, lower heat to medium-low, cover, and cook for 10 minutes. Remove from heat.

Remove parsley and discard. Strain out vegetables; return broth to the pot. Purée the vegetables in a blender or food processor and add to broth.

Remove the cores from the tomatoes. Halve them, gently squeeze out seeds, and coarsely chop. Add them to the pot along with the tomato paste. Bring mixture to a boil, lower heat, and stir to break up tomatoes. Simmer 10 to 20 minutes, or until soup begins to thicken. Watch carefully; don't allow it to burn.

Add the broth and simmer for 30 minutes, stirring occasionally. Taste for seasonings and adjust as necessary.

Serve in individual heated soup bowls garnished with fresh herbs.

AFTERTHOUGHT: This is a deep, dark secret, so keep this quiet: Add 2 or 3 drops of red food coloring at the end to make it the color tomato soup used to be.

BASQUE SOUP

Serves six

The Basques have a firm grip on making soup, and this is one of the best.

1 pound salt cod
¼ cup olive oil
2 large onions, coarsely chopped
2 medium leeks, white part only, coarsely chopped
2 large sweet red peppers, cored, seeded, and cut into 1-inch squares
1 large green pepper, cored, seeded, and cut into 1-inch squares
2 medium-size ripe tomatoes, peeled, seeded, and coarsely chopped

2 large garlic cloves, minced
4 medium potatoes, scrubbed, unpeeled, and cut into eighths
1 bay leaf
½ teaspoon dried thyme
Pinch of saffron
Freshly ground black pepper
½ cup apple cider
8 cups cold water
4 slices French bread, made into 1-inch Garlic Croutons (page 67)
12 oil-cured black olives, pitted and slivered

Soak cod overnight in 4 quarts cold water, changing the water two or three times. Drain. Cut cod into 1-inch chunks and reserve.

Heat olive oil in a large soup pot over low to moderate heat. Add onions and leeks and sauté until onions begin to turn translucent, about 5 minutes. Add peppers and sauté for 5 minutes. Add tomatoes and garlic and cook 2 minutes longer.

Add cod and remaining ingredients except bread and olives and bring to a boil. Lower heat, cover, and simmer until the fish and potatoes are tender, about 20 minutes. Taste for seasoning and adjust as needed.

Ladle soup into six warm individual soup bowls. Top with a few croutons and a sprinkling of slivered olives.

AFTERTHOUGHT: This soup would be splendid served with thin toasted French bread slices and Garlic Tapenade (page 9).

GILDED LILY SOUP

Serves eight

What a lovely first course this is.

4 *large shallots, chopped*
1 *onion, chopped*
1 *pound medium leeks, white part only, well washed and chopped*
4 *tablespoons butter*
2 *tablespoons peanut oil*
1 *small potato, peeled and diced*
1 *cup dry white wine*

8 *cups chicken broth, homemade or canned*
Salt
Freshly ground black pepper
1 *pint heavy cream*
1 *pound mushrooms, sliced*
1 *small bunch fresh chives, minced*

In a large pot, cook the shallots, onion, and leeks in 2 tablespoons of the butter and the oil over moderate heat until softened, about 10 minutes.

Add the potato, wine, broth, and salt and pepper to taste. Bring to a boil, lower heat, and simmer the mixture for 30 minutes.

In a blender or food processor, blend the soup in batches until it is smooth and return it to the pot. Add cream and heat slowly until it is hot.

Meanwhile, lightly sauté the mushrooms in remaining 2 tablespoons butter. Season to taste with salt and pepper.

Serve soup in individual heated soup bowls, garnished with mushrooms and a drift of minced chives.

❧

WOLFGANG PUCK'S SOUPE AU PISTOU
(Vegetable Soup with Sweet Basil)

Serves six

Considerable skill is called for in order to cut the vegetables into small dice, called *brunoise* in the French version. If you lack the skill, don't shed any tears; cut them as neatly as you can and get on with it. The most important thing is to start with a rich flavorful chicken broth. Add the freshest vegetables the market affords, cook the soup lightly so that the vegetables retain their color and flavors, and be rewarded with a bright, fresh soup, the essence of summer.

2 small leeks, white part only
1 large potato, peeled
1 small onion
2 celery stalks
1 medium zucchini
12 green beans
2 medium carrots
6 tablespoons olive oil
3 tablespoons water

2 quarts chicken broth
6 ripe tomatoes, peeled and
  seeded
4 garlic cloves, peeled
30 fresh basil leaves, washed
  and dried
Salt
½ teaspoon freshly ground pepper

Cut vegetables into 1/4-inch dice.

In a 6-quart stockpot, combine 3 tablespoons of the olive oil with the 3 tablespoons water. Add the vegetables and sauté over medium-low heat until all the water evaporates. Do not brown the vegetables.

Add the broth and bring to a boil. Cook at a gentle boil for 30 minutes.

Meanwhile, make a purée with the tomatoes, garlic, basil leaves, and remaining 3 tablespoons of olive oil. Add the purée to the cooked soup and stir thoroughly. Do not boil again.

Season to taste with salt and pepper. Serve hot or cold.

POTAGE CRESSONIÈRE

Serves four to six

An elegant, fresh soup. Serve hot or chilled.

2 tablespoons butter
2 leeks, well washed and
  trimmed of all but 1½ inches
  of green tops, cut into small
  pieces
1 bunch watercress, washed and
  dried (reserve a few nice
  leaves)

1 quart chicken broth
2 potatoes, peeled and diced
1 cup heavy cream
1 tablespoon sour cream
Salt
Freshly ground black pepper

Melt half the butter in a large heavy saucepan. Add leeks and watercress and sauté for 10 minutes.

Add broth, bring to a boil, and then add potatoes. Continue to boil until all vegetables are cooked.

Place soup in a food processor, and whirl to a fine purée. Return to saucepan and add cream, sour cream, and remaining butter and heat to a slight boil. Adjust seasonings.

Serve in individual soup bowls garnished with reserved watercress leaves.

LEEK SOUP

Serves six generously

From the Basque communities in California comes this aromatic soup, as flavorful as it is easily made.

4–5 strips bacon, sliced into
　　1/4-inch pieces
6 medium leeks (about 2
　　pounds), well washed and
　　trimmed, leaving only 1 1/2 to
　　2 inches of green top, and cut
　　into 1/2-inch slices
1 medium onion, chopped
2 garlic cloves, minced
2 tablespoons flour (Wondra
　　works like a charm)
2 quarts beef broth (homemade, I
　　hope)

4 medium all-purpose potatoes,
　　peeled and cut into 1-inch
　　cubes
1 teaspoon herbes de Provence
Salt
Freshly ground black pepper

GARNISH

6 heart-shaped croutons, sautéed
　　in olive oil until golden
1 small sweet red pepper, cored,
　　seeded, and cut into small dice
2 tablespoons snipped chives

Sauté the bacon in a soup kettle until it is lightly browned, 6 to 8 minutes.

Add the leeks, onion, and garlic and cook, stirring frequently, until the leeks are tender, about 10 minutes. Sprinkle the flour over the vegetables and stir for a couple of minutes.

Add the beef broth, potatoes, and herbs and bring to a boil. Reduce the heat and simmer until the potatoes are tender, about 20 minutes. Season with salt and a few grindings of pepper.

Divide the soup among six heated soup bowls. Garnish each with a heart-shaped crouton, a portion of sweet red pepper, and a sprinkling of chives.

AFTERTHOUGHT:　At the last minute drop in a handful of shredded fresh spinach leaves. Don't cook them, just let them soften and retain their color.

ROMAN LEEK SOUP

A soup recipe written by Langham, an Englishman, in 1579.

"Nature to restore, eat of this Soupe first & last [morning and evening]: Marrow Bones with the flesh, Leekes, Pepper, Ginger, Cinnamon & Nutmeg."

꿢

COCK-A-LEEKIE

Serves four to six

This soup with its intriguing name is an old favorite from Scotland.

As for the chicken, what we used to call stewing hens now have to be ordered from specialty shops. The young stuff available in the supermarkets is inclined to fall apart when cooked in soup—spurn them. Look for a matronly bird with some substance for this fine, rich soup.

1 stewing chicken, about 4 pounds	*8 peppercorns*
	Chicken broth to cover
3 pounds leeks, well washed and trimmed of all but 1½ inches of green tops	*2 medium potatoes, peeled and coarsely chopped*
1 large onion, quartered	*½ pound pitted prunes (optional)*
6 sprigs parsley	*1 cup heavy cream (optional)*
½ teaspoon dried thyme	*¼ cup chopped parsley*
1 bay leaf	

Remove excess fat from chicken and discard, or save and render (see page 173). Remove giblets and save for another use. (You may like to add the heart and gizzard to the pot, but don't add the liver.)

Put the chicken in a large casserole and surround with half the leeks and the onion. Tie parsley, thyme, bay leaf and peppercorns in cheesecloth and add to the pot. Pour in broth to cover and bring to a boil. Reduce heat and simmer, partly covered, for 2 hours, or until tender.

Remove leeks, onion, and chicken (including heart and gizzard if you used them) from broth. Discard bouquet garni. Cool chicken and remove meat from bones, discarding skin. Set aside. Degrease broth.

Purée leeks and onion in a food processor or blender. Return to pot. Cut remaining leeks into 1/2-inch rounds and add to broth with chopped potatoes. Cook until tender, about 20 minutes. Add chicken and optional prunes and simmer another 10 minutes. Stir in cream.

Serve in individual heated soup bowls and garnish with chopped parsley.

AFTERTHOUGHT: If you must buy a teenage bird, simmer it about 1 1/2 hours. Watch closely or it will fall off the bone before you know it.

❧

WELSH LEEK AND POTATO SOUP

Serves four to six

A fine, comforting soup.

4 tablespoons butter or rendered chicken fat (see Afterthoughts)
3 pounds medium leeks, well washed and trimmed of all but 1½ inches of green tops, chopped
2 large onions, chopped
2 carrots, peeled and finely chopped
6–8 medium potatoes, peeled and thickly sliced

2 quarts chicken broth
1 celery top, including leaves
Pinch of dried thyme
1 small bay leaf
Salt
Freshly ground black pepper
2 cups half-and-half or cream
Sour cream
¼ cup minced chives

Melt butter or chicken fat in a large casserole. Add leeks, onions, and carrots and sauté until soft. Do not brown. Add potatoes and cook, stirring with leek mixture, 5 minutes.

Pour in chicken broth. Add celery top, thyme, and bay leaf; season with salt and pepper to taste. Bring to a boil, reduce heat to simmer, and cook until potatoes are tender, 30 to 40 minutes. Discard celery top and bay leaf. (At this point you may cover pot and set aside to mellow a couple of hours—or overnight in the refrigerator.)

Mash potatoes coarsely with a potato masher, but leave lumps. Add cream and check seasonings. Heat but do not boil. Serve in individual heated soup bowls, garnished with sour cream and chives, and a sprinkling of cracklings, if desired.

AFTERTHOUGHTS: To render chicken fat: Remove excess fat and fatty skin from bird. Cut fatty skin into small pieces. In a heavy saucepan render chicken fat and skin over low to moderate heat. If you wish to make skin into cracklings, reheat them until crisp in a small skillet. Drain on paper towels. Use as garnish.

This soup will become silken vichyssoise if you omit the carrot, and purée the soup after the potatoes are tender so that it is totally blended. Combine it with 2 cups heavy cream, chill well, and serve in equally cold individual soup bowls garnished with a drift of minced chives.

HALIBUT SOUP

Serves four generously

Just the thing on a blustery evening; but remember this: don't overcook the green veggies, allow them to retain their color and texture. Don't cook the hell out of the fish either; in other words, this soup should not cook too long!

3–4 *medium leeks, white part*
  only, sliced thin
2 *small carrots, peeled and sliced*
  thin
1 *large garlic clove, chopped fine*
2 *tablespoons olive oil*
1 *cup dry white wine*
1 *quart fish stock, clam juice, or*
  chicken broth
2 *potatoes, peeled and diced*

1 *turnip, peeled and diced*
2 *zucchini, sliced*
4 *kale leaves, cut into julienne*
  (use scissors)
1½ *pounds halibut, cut into*
  large chunks
Salt
Freshly ground black pepper
Snipped fresh dill and parsley
Thin slices of lemon

In a large casserole, sauté the leeks, carrots, and garlic in olive oil until softened. Do not allow them to brown. Add the wine and reduce by half. Add the stock, potatoes, and turnip and simmer until the vegetables are tender.

About 10 minutes before serving, add the zucchini and kale. About 5 minutes before, add the fish. Simmer until *just* cooked through.

Correct the seasonings and serve at once, garnished with the herbs and a slice of lemon.

Of soup and love, the first is best.
—Spanish proverb

MUSSEL SOUP

Serves six

The bottom of the soup bowl is revealed very quickly when you fill it with the "soup of the evening, beautiful soup."

3 pounds mussels	*½ teaspoon dried thyme*
½ pound carrots, peeled	*1 pint heavy cream*
½ pound slender leeks, well washed and trimmed of all but 1½ inches of green tops	*Salt*
	Freshly ground black pepper
	Cayenne
½ pound celery, washed and trimmed	*Lemon juice*
	2 tablespoons diced sweet yellow pepper
1 cup dry white wine	
3 cups fish stock, clam juice, or Knorr instant fish bouillon	*2 tablespoons diced sweet red pepper*
1 tablespoon butter	*Snipped fresh chives*
½ teaspoon saffron	

Wash mussels carefully; remove sand and beards.

Coarsely chop approximately 1/4 pound each of the carrots, leeks, and celery. Place mussels in a large casserole with the chopped vegetables, wine, and fish stock. Bring to a boil and cook 5 minutes. Remove mussels and set aside. Strain broth through cheesecloth and reserve.

Cut remaining vegetables in *brunoise* (first julienne, then tiny dice). Heat butter in a large saucepan and add vegetables, saffron, and thyme and cook slowly 10 minutes.

Add heavy cream and bring to a boil. Lower heat and simmer 5 minutes, or until mixture reduces slightly. Add reserved broth from mussels and reduce slightly once again over high heat. Lower heat to barest simmer and keep warm.

Shuck mussels and add to soup. Season to taste with salt and pepper, cayenne, and lemon juice. Serve in individual heated soup bowls, garnished with finely diced peppers and a sprinkling of chives.

AFTERTHOUGHT: Buy the New Zealand mussels. They're big and fat and a gorgeous color.

SPRING SOUP

Serves six

The essence of spring and one of my all-time favorites. Equally good served hot or chilled.

3 tablespoons butter	*3 cups chicken broth*
1½ cups thinly sliced scallions	*½ cup heavy cream*
1 heaping tablespoon flour	*1 cucumber, peeled and thinly*
2 tablespoons Dijon mustard	*sliced*
Salt	*Watercress leaves*
Freshly ground black pepper	*Sour cream*

Melt butter at low to medium heat. Sauté scallions until they are just softened and bright green. Sprinkle with flour and stir well. Blend in mustard, lower heat, and simmer for a minute or two. Taste and adjust seasonings.

Raise heat to high and whisk in chicken broth. Bring to a boil and remove from heat.

Just before serving, whisk in the cream and heat through. Divide cucumber slices among six warm soup bowls. Ladle soup over them. Garnish with a leaf of watercress and a dollop of sour cream and serve at once.

ENTRÉES

❧

CHICKEN IN THE POT WITH GREEN SHALLOT SAUCE

Serves four

Janis's delight. Once you get this all together you can leave it to its own devices, simmering away happily. Arranged on its platter, it is a lavish, aromatic presentation; the pretty green sauce sets everything off perfectly.

1 roasting chicken, about 3½ pounds (save liver and heart and mince)
4 ounces prosciutto, minced
1 medium onion, minced
2 garlic cloves, minced
2 extra chicken livers, finely chopped
¼ cup finely chopped parsley
½ teaspoon dried thyme and marjoram, or rosemary, or chervil
or
1 tablespoon fresh
1 egg, beaten
1 cup soft bread crumbs, packed
Freshly ground black pepper
3 quarts strong chicken broth plus enough water to just cover chicken, if necessary

Pinch each of ground cloves, nutmeg, cayenne, and ginger
Salt
1 rounded tablespoon tomato paste
1 large garlic clove, chopped
8–12 tiny red potatoes, scrubbed, unpeeled
8–10 tiny boiling onions, peeled, whole
4 large carrots, scrubbed and cut into 2-inch lengths
1 small cabbage, cored and quartered
Green Shallot Sauce (recipe follows)

Remove giblets from chicken. Wipe out cavity with damp paper towels. Set aside.

Combine prosciutto, onion, garlic, livers, heart, parsley, herbs, egg, bread crumbs, and pepper to taste. Stuff chicken, sew up openings, and truss securely.

Place the chicken in a casserole or pot large enough to hold it comfortably. Cover with broth, to which you have added spices, salt, tomato paste, and garlic, and bring to a boil. Lower heat and simmer, cover ajar, until chicken is tender, about 1 1/2 hours. Take care not to overcook the bird.

Meanwhile, boil potatoes, onions, and carrots until just tender. Drain and set aside.

During the last 20 minutes of simmering the chicken, slip the cooked vegetables and cabbage quarters into the broth. At the end of cooking time, remove chicken from stock, discard strings, and cut into quarters. Slice stuffing. Arrange chicken, stuffing, and vegetables attractively on a large heated platter. Spoon a few tablespoons of hot broth over all. Serve immediately with Green Shallot Sauce. (You may want to strain and reserve broth for another use —it's delicious.)

GREEN SHALLOT SAUCE

3 hard-boiled egg yolks
2 tablespoons sherry wine
   vinegar
½ cup olive oil
¼ cup minced parsley
2 or 3 large shallots, minced
1 small garlic clove, minced

1 tablespoon minced capers
Salt
Freshly ground pepper
Dash of cayenne
Squeeze of lemon
1 teaspoon anchovy paste
   (optional)

Combine egg yolks and vinegar in a blender. Add olive oil bit by bit, blending all the while until emulsified.

Add parsley, shallots, garlic, capers, salt and pepper to taste, cayenne, a bit of lemon juice, and anchovy paste. Blend again. Adjust seasonings. (This sauce may be prepared a day in advance. Beat well before serving.)

FISH AND SHALLOTS BAKED
IN PARCHMENT

Serves 6

Light, pretty, and easy to prepare.

2 tablespoons balsamic or sherry wine vinegar	*6 red snapper (or bass) fillets*
	Fruity olive oil
1 cup thinly (that's thinly) sliced shallots	*Salt*
	Freshly ground black pepper
1 large head butter lettuce or large spinach leaves, well washed	*6 sprigs fresh thyme, rosemary, dill, or tarragon*
	Beurre Blanc (page 216)

Combine vinegar and shallots in a small frying pan and cook over moderate heat for about 5 minutes, or until soft. Set aside.

Preheat oven to 350° F.

Dip large outer leaves of butter lettuce into a large saucepan of boiling water just long enough to soften them—a few seconds. Hold stem ends of leaves with tongs or fingertips (if brave). Hold them over the pot to drain and then lay them on paper towels to blot dry.

Wipe fillets with damp paper towels. Rub them with olive oil and sprinkle with salt and pepper to taste. Cover one side of each fillet with a lettuce leaf (remove tough stem if there is one) and lay it, leaf side down, on a sheet of kitchen parchment (or aluminum foil) about twice as large as the fillet.

Divide the shallot mixture among the six fillets, spooning it evenly over each piece. Lay an herb sprig on each serving and cover with another lettuce leaf, overlapping edges to seal. Fold over parchment (or foil) and crimp edges so no steam will escape.

Put fillets on a large baking sheet and place in the preheated oven for about 12 minutes, longer if the fillets are very thick. Serve immediately, and let your guests break open the parchment. (If you have used foil, you probably will want to remove it yourself before serving). Pass a sauceboat of beurre blanc.

SHRIMP BALL CURRY

Serves four

Serve this spicy Thai dish with boiled rice, or as an appetizer as part of an exotic feed.

½ pound raw shrimp, peeled and minced
½ pound raw pork, minced
2 garlic cloves, minced
1 teaspoon minced fresh ginger
1 teaspoon cornstarch
1 teaspoon salt
1 tablespoon peanut oil
½ small onion, sliced thin

1 teaspoon crushed dried hot red pepper
½ teaspoon turmeric
½ cup chopped tomato, fresh or canned
1½ cups broth or water
1 teaspoon Thai fish sauce (nam pla)
¼ cup chopped fresh coriander

Combine the shrimp, pork, half the garlic, ginger, cornstarch, and 1/2 teaspoon of the salt in a bowl. Mix until well blended. Shape heaping teaspoonfuls into round balls.

Heat the oil in a medium saucepan. Add the onion, hot pepper, turmeric, and remaining garlic. Stir-fry over medium heat until the onion is softened but not browned, about 2 minutes. Add the tomato and broth. Bring to a boil, then simmer for 5 minutes.

Stir in fish sauce and remaining salt. Add the shrimp balls; they will not be covered by the sauce. Cook, uncovered, over moderately low heat for 10 minutes. Stir in the coriander and continue to cook for 5 minutes.

VIETNAMESE TOMATOES STUFFED WITH PORK AND SHALLOTS

Serves six

I served these tomatoes at room temperature with the sauce very hot, and they were fabulous. They were part of a gorgeous dinner of calf's liver sautéed in butter, the skillet deglazed with a dash of balsamic vinegar and red wine, well reduced. The plates were finished with florets of blanched, room-temperature broccoli and Indonesian Crisp Onion Flakes (page 126). We drank a nice young claret and had great big strawberries, unadorned, for dessert.

6 medium tomatoes, ripe but still firm
2 garlic cloves, minced
2 large shallots, minced
2 scallions, chopped
½ pound ground pork
1 teaspoon sugar
1 tablespoon Vietnamese fish sauce (nuoc mam; see Afterthoughts)
Freshly ground black pepper

Dash of salt
¼ cup vegetable oil

SAUCE
⅓ cup water
1 tablespoon Oriental fish sauce
2 teaspoons sugar
1 garlic clove, peeled and crushed
2 teaspoons tomato paste
4–5 teaspoons light soy sauce
Cilantro sprigs for garnish

Cut the tops from the tomatoes and scoop out the centers, taking care not to puncture the bottoms. Dry the insides carefully with paper towels. This is important; the stuffing will stay inside if the tomato shell is dry.

In a small bowl combine the garlic, shallots, scallions, pork, sugar, fish sauce, pepper, and salt with your hands or a spoon (hands work better here). Divide the mixture into six equal portions and stuff the tomatoes firmly, flattening the stuffing in the top of each tomato.

Heat the vegetable oil in a sauté pan or wok over high heat. Add the tomatoes, stuffing side down, reduce heat to medium, cover, and cook for 5 to 6 minutes. Turn the tomatoes right side up, cover, and cook another 5 or 6 minutes. Remove the tomatoes to a serving dish and keep warm while you make the sauce.

Combine all ingredients for the sauce (except cilantro) in a small saucepan and blend well. Bring to a boil, stirring frequently, and cook for a minute or so. Remove the garlic and pour the boiling sauce over the tomatoes. Garnish with sprigs of cilantro and serve.

AFTERTHOUGHTS: You may substitute Thai fish sauce, nam pla, for the Vietnamese, if it is unavailable, but there is no substitute for fish sauce itself. It has a subtle flavor and adds a touch of the mysterious East to many memorable dishes.

Can you imagine how good this filling would be rolled up in lightly blanched leaves of red cabbage and baked in a covered casserole with a cup or so of chicken broth? Serve the rolls with the same sauce, and cilantro sprigs or minced chives.

Or try equal parts of ground turkey and pork. Serve with stir-fried spinach and tiny peas, and, dare I say, mashed potatoes. Rice would be very good, of course, but my hands-down preference is always mashed potatoes.

Wait a minute! Try this one: Sauté 1 cup ground turkey until brown in a couple of tablespoons of peanut oil. Add a tablespoon of cornstarch and combine well, then add the same amounts of garlic, shallots, scallions, sugar, salt and pepper, and fish sauce as required for the tomato stuffing. Wrap heaping teaspoonfuls of the mixture into Napa cabbage or romaine leaves and steam for 5 minutes over boiling water, or until just heated through. Serve as hors d'oeuvres, with or without the sauce, or drop them in clear chicken broth.

How about using the filling for fried won tons?

Stuff this mixture into bright green Anaheim chilies. Don't roast the chilies; just remove stems and seeds. Fill and sauté over moderate heat until brown on both sides. Add a little water, cover, and cook until filling is no longer pink, about 10 minutes.

TONGUE WITH MADEIRA SAUCE

Serves six to eight

This is a fine dish: smoky, aromatic, and meltingly tender. Even people who think they don't like tongue will be enthusiastic fans if you serve it thus.

2 calves' tongues, about 1 pound
   each, smoked or fresh
Salt
⅓ cup dried currants
½ cup Madeira
2 tablespoons unsalted butter
4 small shallots, minced
2 garlic cloves, peeled and
   mashed
1½ cups beef broth

½ cup red wine
2 teaspoons currant jelly
2 strips orange peel, about 3
   inches long, cut into fine
   julienne
1 teaspoon Dijon mustard
1 tablespoon cornstarch
Juice of 1 small lemon
Freshly ground black pepper

In a large saucepan, cook smoked tongues in boiling water for forty-five minutes. (If the tongues are fresh, add 1 tablespoon salt to the water.) Refresh under cold water and peel if possible. If the tongues do not peel easily, continue with the recipe and peel just before slicing.

Soak the currants in the Madeira for at least 3 hours. Drain and set aside, reserving Madeira.

Melt the butter in a medium saucepan over moderate heat. Add the shallots and garlic and cook until tender, about 4 minutes. Add 1 1/4 cups of the beef broth, the reserved Madeira, red wine, and currant jelly and bring to a boil. Cook over moderately high heat until the jelly is melted and the mixture is slightly reduced.

Preheat oven to 350°F.

Strain the mixture and discard the shallots and garlic. Return to the saucepan. Add orange peel, mustard, and currants. Mix the cornstarch into the remaining 1/4 cup beef broth and whisk it into the sauce. Lower heat and simmer a few minutes.

Add the lemon juice, taste for seasoning; add salt and pepper if you think it needs it. By now the sauce should be shiny and reduced to about 1 1/2 cups. Remove from heat and set aside.

Cut the tongue into 1/2-inch diagonal slices and arrange them in a single overlapping layer in an oiled, ovenproof gratin dish or shallow casserole. Pour the Madeira mixture over it, making sure that the entire tongue is graced with the sauce.

Cover loosely with foil, place in the preheated oven, and allow to simmer gently for 45 minutes to 1 hour.

AFTERTHOUGHTS: Lightly sautéed chicken livers are a knock-out served with this sauce.

Baked ham slices heated in this sauce have found their natural home.

❧

GILDED LILY TART

Serves four

Some enlightened tinkering has gone on here with the old stand-by, spanakopitas; and not a moment too soon. Crisp and puffy with a complex flavor, it's a pretty dish to set before the king—or anyone else you favor. Good hot or at room temperature. It may also go along on a picnic, given reasonable care.

2 tablespoons butter
2 medium leeks, white part only, well washed and sliced thin (or 1 medium onion, halved and sliced thin
4 medium scallions, white part only, sliced thin
1 garlic clove, minced
2 packages frozen chopped spinach, defrosted, squeezed dry
¼ cup finely diced prosciutto
Freshly ground black pepper

Sprinkling of freshly grated nutmeg
2 large eggs
½ cup coarsely grated Gruyère cheese
¼ cup crumbled Gorgonzola cheese
2 tablespoons freshly grated Parmesan cheese
⅔ cup ricotta cheese
10 sheets filo dough, defrosted (see Afterthoughts)
½ cup clarified butter

Melt the 2 tablespoons butter in a heavy skillet over moderate heat. Add leeks and scallions and sauté until softened, stirring often. Do not brown. Add garlic, spinach, prosciutto, pepper to taste, and nutmeg and cook, stirring frequently, until spinach is tender, about 5 minutes. Remove from heat and set aside.

Preheat oven to 375°F.

Combine eggs and cheeses in a large bowl. Add spinach mixture (leave any cooking liquid behind) and blend well.

Unfold filo sheets and cover with a damp tea towel. Rub a baking sheet with a bit of clarified butter. Remove 1 sheet, keeping remaining sheets covered to prevent drying, and lay on baking sheet. Brush filo carefully with clarified butter, cover with a second sheet, and brush with more butter. Continue layering sheets and butter until 5 sheets have been prepared. Spoon spinach mixture onto center of top sheet, mounding slightly into a rectangular shape. Cover filling with another sheet of filo, and brush with butter as before. Stack 4 more sheets, buttering all but the last one. Roll and fold the long sides of the filo toward center, then fold in ends, enclosing filling completely. Brush top and sides of pie with remaining butter.

Bake 20 minutes in preheated oven, or until dough is golden brown and crisp. Transfer to a wire rack to cool a few minutes before cutting into servings.

AFTERTHOUGHTS: Filo, or phyllo, is the tissue-thin dough common to the Middle East. Frozen filo is available in 1-pound packages in most large supermarkets or in Middle Eastern or specialty markets.

Let it defrost in its original wrapper in your refrigerator for a day or so, or overnight. If wrapped well after opening, defrosted filo will keep in the refrigerator for about a month.

Before you use it, make sure it is completely defrosted, and keep it covered with a damp towel. Let it stand for about 15 minutes, covered, to make it easier to handle. Use it in whole sheets for pies as above, or cut into triangles or rectangles to enclose fillings for hors d'oeuvres.

LEEK AND RED PEPPER TART

Serves four to six

A pleasing dish for a light Sunday supper.

3 tablespoons unsalted butter
2 cups thinly sliced leeks, white
    part only

4 shallots, sliced thin
1 garlic clove, minced
1 teaspoon minced fresh rosemary

2 tablespoons minced fresh
  parsley
1 large sweet red pepper, cored,
  seeded, and diced fairly small
Freshly ground black pepper

Dash of nutmeg
3 eggs
1 pint heavy cream
½ cup grated Gruyère cheese
9-inch prebaked pie shell

Preheat oven to 350°F.

Melt the butter in a skillet and cook the leeks, shallots, and garlic over moderate to low heat for 10 to 15 minutes, or until they are softened and golden. Blend in the rosemary, parsley, diced red pepper, a grinding or two of pepper, and a dash of nutmeg. Taste for seasonings; add what it needs. Cool.

Beat the eggs lightly, add the cream, and blend well. When the leek mixture has cooled, add it to the egg mixture. Pour into a baked pie shell and sprinkle with grated cheese.

Place the tart in the center of the middle rack of the oven until the custard is set, approximately 40 minutes. Serve warm.

QUICHE, MA MAISON

Serves six to eight

There is really no reason to make any other. This is the best quiche there is.

Puff pastry for one quiche
  (homemade or frozen)
1 egg yolk, lightly beaten
½ pound bacon, diced
¼ cup minced chives
2 shallots, minced
½ cup coarsely grated Gruyère
  cheese

7 large eggs
3 cups cream
¼ teaspoon nutmeg
¼ teaspoon salt
½ teaspoon freshly ground white
  pepper

Preheat oven to 350°F.

Line a buttered 10-inch quiche pan with puff pastry, but do not trim the edges. Line the pastry with aluminum foil, fill with aluminum pellets or dried beans, and bake 15 minutes. Remove from oven and remove beans and foil. Brush bottom of the crust with egg yolk and return to oven for 10 minutes, or until lightly browned.

Meanwhile, cook the diced bacon until crisp. Drain on paper towels.

Trim edges of shell. Sprinkle bacon, chives, shallots, and cheese over bottom of shell.

Beat the eggs and remaining ingredients until blended. Pour into shell. Place quiche pan on the center rack of the preheated oven and bake 40 minutes, or until quiche has puffed and browned.

GRATIN OF SCALLIONS, SAVOYARD

Serves six

How about a Ramos fizz, this satisfying dish, some meaningful muffins, and lots of fresh fruit to get Sunday morning off to a good start?

12 large scallions	*2 large eggs plus 2 egg yolks*
2 tablespoons butter	*Salt*
6 thin slices boiled ham, halved	*Freshly ground black pepper*
1 cup milk	*½ cup grated cheese (Gruyère*
1 cup whipping cream	*and a little Parmesan)*

Wash the scallions and trim them into 6-inch lengths. Arrange them in a single layer in a large heavy skillet. Dot with butter and add water to cover. Place over medium heat, cover, and poach until tender, about 10 minutes. Drain thoroughly on paper towels.

Preheat oven to 375°F.

Lightly butter a shallow baking dish. Wrap each scallion in a half-slice of ham and arrange in a single layer in the prepared dish.

In a bowl, combine milk, cream, eggs and egg yolks, salt and pepper to taste, and blend thoroughly. Pour over scallions and top with grated cheese. Bake 45 minutes, or until top is browned and a knife inserted near the center comes out clean. Serve immediately.

AFTERTHOUGHT: This recipe works equally well with young leeks.

VEGETABLES

BLACKENED LEEKS AND RED ONIONS VINAIGRETTE

Serves four

Next time you fire up the grill, remember this one. It's a stunner and, happily, may be prepared in advance over the coals. Good stuff.

8–10 slender young leeks, well washed and trimmed of all but 1 inch of green tops

2 large red onions, peeled and quartered
Mustard Vinaigrette (page 52)

Cook leeks in boiling water to cover until just barely tender. Drain.

Steam onion quarters over boiling water until barely tender. Remove carefully. When cool enough to handle, thread onto bamboo skewers.

Place leeks and skewered onions in 1 layer in a shallow Pyrex dish. Pour Mustard Vinaigrette over them and let them marinate at least 2 hours at room temperature.

Place leeks and onions on a grill over hot coals and roast them for about 5 minutes, brushing them with leftover vinaigrette as they cook. Turn them frequently. Serve with grilled meats.

LEEKS AND PEAS, BASQUE STYLE

Serves four

Don't miss this one!

2 ounces prosciutto, minced
1 small sweet red pepper, cored,
   seeded, and slivered
1 garlic clove, minced
1 tablespoon olive oil

3 slender leeks, halved
   lengthwise, well washed and
   trimmed, leaving only 1½ to
   2 inches of green top, sliced
   into 3-inch julienne
1 package frozen peas, defrosted
Freshly ground black pepper

In a saucepan over moderate heat, sauté the prosciutto, red pepper, and garlic in olive oil for about 5 minutes.

Add the julienned leeks and cook, covered, for about 5 minutes, stirring frequently, until the leeks are just tender.

Uncover and stir in peas and a grinding or two of pepper, and heat through. Taste for seasonings and serve immediately.

SUPREME OF LEEKS AND POTATOES GRATINÉE

Serves four to six

This one is well named; it is superb. The silken leeks in their creamy sauce combine perfectly with the texture of the freshly baked potatoes and the whisper of nutmeg. It has another advantage—it may be put together several hours before you plan to serve it; no last-minute hassle.

4 medium-large Idaho potatoes,
   scrubbed and oiled
8 tablespoons butter
6–8 young leeks, trimmed of all
   but 1 inch of green top, well
   washed, sliced in half the long
   way and cut into ½-inch slices
3 tablespoons all-purpose flour

2 cups milk
1 teaspoon salt
Freshly ground black pepper
¼ teaspoon ground nutmeg
¼ cup minced parsley
½ cup grated Gruyère cheese
Snipped chives for garnish

Bake the potatoes in a preheated 400°F oven until a fork pierces them easily, about 50 minutes. Set aside.

Meanwhile, melt the butter in a heavy saucepan and sauté the leeks until they are *just* tender, about 5 minutes. Do not allow them to brown. Sprinkle with flour and stir. Add milk, salt, pepper to taste, and nutmeg, and let the sauce simmer for about 5 minutes, stirring gently. Don't overcook the leeks here; be kind. Stir in the parsley and remove from heat.

Lay the potatoes on their sides and cut a slice off the top. Scoop them out right into the sauce, breaking them up a little, but leaving lots of lumps. (I'll bet that's the first time any cookbook ever said that to you.) Mix gently and pour into a well-buttered gratin dish. Do not smooth the top.

About 45 minutes before you want to serve the gratiné, preheat oven to 450°F, then sprinkle the mixture with cheese and slip the dish into the hot oven. When the potatoes are very hot and the cheese is golden and crusty, (about 20 minutes), it is ready to serve, garnished with the snipped chives.

AFTERTHOUGHT: Try this: Cut the baked potato skins into thinnish slivers and fry them in hot oil until they are very crisp. Use them for a finishing touch.

ROASTED LEEKS

Serves two or three

Fast and delicious.

8 slender leeks (thumb-size, if   *Olive oil*
possible), well washed and   *Salt*
trimmed of all but 1 inch of   *Freshly ground black pepper*
green tops

Preheat oven to 450°F.

Pat leeks dry with paper towels. Place them in one layer on a large sheet of heavy-duty aluminum foil. Rub each one with olive oil and sprinkle with salt and pepper to taste. Tightly close the foil and place the package on a baking sheet.

Bake 5 minutes in the preheated oven. Turn the package over and bake 5 minutes more.

Serve them lukewarm with your best vinaigrette dressing, complete with garlic and fresh herbs.

AFTERTHOUGHT: These leeks can also be roasted under the broiler or grilled outside over the coals. Broiling time will be the same as for baking; grilling takes about 10 minutes to a side.

JAPANESE LEEKS WITH MISO

Serves four

Satori for leeks.

¼ cup red miso (see   *2 tablespoons vegetable oil*
Afterthought)   *10 slender leeks, cut into 1½-*
1 tablespoon honey   *inch diagonals*
2 tablespoons mirin   *2 tablespoons toasted sesame seeds*
2 tablespoons water

Preheat oven to 400°F.

Combine miso, honey, mirin, and water in a small bowl.

Heat oil in a wok or skillet. Toss in leeks and stir-fry until just tender, 2 to 3 minutes. Pour in miso sauce and simmer a few minutes until just beginning to thicken.

Pour leeks and sauce into a small casserole or gratin and roast in the oven about 25 minutes, or until glazed. Sprinkle with sesame seeds and serve.

AFTERTHOUGHT: Miso is available in many supermarkets and most Oriental markets.

LEEKS NICOISE

Serves six

A lovely dish for a summer's evening.

3–4 large ripe tomatoes	*½ teaspoon dried thyme*
½ cup olive oil	*Salt*
2 garlic cloves, minced	*Freshly ground black pepper*
2 tablespoons minced parsley	*12 leeks, well washed and*
4–5 leaves fresh basil, coarsely	*trimmed of all but 2 inches of*
chopped	*green tops*
1 small bay leaf	*8–10 Greek olives*

Immerse the tomatoes in boiling water for 30 seconds. Peel, quarter, and set aside.

Heat oil in a large skillet over low heat. Add garlic and parsley and cook 1 minute. Add tomatoes, basil, bay leaf, thyme, and salt and pepper to taste. Cover and cook slowly for 5 minutes.

Add leeks to skillet; they should fit snugly in a single layer. Cover and braise for 10 minutes, or until tender. Test occasionally with a sharp knife. Transfer leeks to a serving plate with a slotted spoon.

Increase heat and cook sauce until it thickens. Taste for seasonings. Spoon sauce over leeks and garnish with olives. Allow vegetables to cool slightly before serving, or serve at room temperature.

AFTERTHOUGHT: No leeks? Use scallions.

LEEKS GRATINÉE

Serves four

A savory presentation of leeks. If leeks aren't to be found, scallions will do just fine.

1 pound leeks, well washed and trimmed, or 4–5 bunches of scallions
¼ pound fresh mushrooms, sliced
3 tablespoons butter
⅓ cup minced ham
1 can (14½ ounces) whole tomatoes, drained, chopped, and drained again

Salt
Freshly ground black pepper
1 cup grated Cheddar cheese
2 tablespoons freshly grated Parmesan cheese

Preheat broiler.

Slice leeks into 1/2-inch rounds and cook them along with the mushrooms in the butter for about 10 minutes, or until just tender.

Mix in.the ham and tomatoes. Season to taste with salt and pepper.

Place the mixture in a well-buttered 1-quart casserole. Top with the cheeses and place under the preheated broiler until the cheese is bubbly and slightly brown.

AFTERTHOUGHT: A teaspoon of fresh or 1/2 teaspoon dried marjoram would be nice.

LILIES OF THE KITCHEN, GRATINÉE

Serves six

This dish has it all—*all* the delicious lilies!

½ pound shallots, peeled and chopped
1 large brown onion, halved lengthwise and sliced thin

3 medium leeks, white part only, well washed and chopped
2 garlic cloves, minced
3 tablespoons butter

1 bag (1 pound) frozen small
   white onions
1 pint heavy cream
Salt
Freshly ground black pepper
Dash of nutmeg

¼ cup minced fresh parsley
3 tablespoons freshly grated
   Parmesan or Romano cheese
2 tablespoons fine white bread
   crumbs

Preheat oven to 475°F.

In a skillet, sauté the shallots, chopped onion, leeks, and garlic in butter until the onion is tender. Add the small white onions and cook, stirring frequently, until they are tender.

Stir in the cream and bring to a boil. Reduce heat and simmer until the cream is thickened. Remove from heat.

Season the mixture with salt and pepper to taste. Stir in nutmeg and parsley, and spoon mixture into a shallow, well-buttered 2-quart baking dish. Sprinkle with the grated cheese and bread crumbs.

Bake in the preheated oven for 15 to 20 minutes, or until the crumbs are golden and the sauce is bubbly. Serve at once.

GREEN BEANS, GASCONY STYLE

Serves six

Leeks, onions, and garlic give their essence to this vegetable dish. It's a nice change; a little something good to eat from the land of d'Artagnan.

3 leeks, white part only, well
   washed and cut into 1½-inch
   slices
1 garlic clove, minced
1½ pounds green beans, washed,
   stemmed, and left whole
2 tablespoons olive oil
2 onions, chopped
3 thin slices ham, diced

1½ tablespoons flour
1 cup chicken broth
1 egg yolk
1 teaspoon sherry wine vinegar
Salt
Freshly ground black pepper
Chopped fresh parsley
Sprigs of fresh thyme

In a large pot of boiling water, blanch the leeks, garlic, and beans for 5 minutes, or until the beans are just tender. Drain and refresh under cold running water. Drain well and set aside.

Heat the olive oil in a frying pan and sauté the onions and ham for 10 minutes. Stirring constantly, sprinkle the flour over the onions, pour in the broth, and continue stirring as the sauce thickens. Keep stirring over moderate heat until the sauce is smooth.

Add the reserved vegetables and simmer for about 5 minutes.

Beat the egg yolk and vinegar together in a small bowl. Gradually beat in 1/2 cup of the hot sauce, a tablespoon at a time, then pour the mixture back into the pan, stirring well. Heat just until the sauce thickens; do not boil.

Taste for seasonings; add salt and pepper as needed. Serve garnished with parsley and sprigs of thyme.

POTATOES, SHALLOTS, AND CÈPES

Serves four

Cèpe is the Gascon word for this wild, earthy mushroom, though they are found all over the world. Here they are combined with another earthy ingredient, namely the potato, to produce a truly soulful dish. The addition of shallots and garlic doesn't hurt either.

½ cup dried cèpes (available in	*½ cup minced shallots*
specialty food stores and,	*1 garlic clove, minced*
increasingly, in supermarkets)	*Salt*
3 pounds boiling potatoes	*Freshly ground black pepper*
2 tablespoons unsalted butter	*1 tablespoon minced fresh chives*
2 tablespoons olive oil	*1 tablespoon minced fresh parsley*

Soak mushrooms in warm water to cover for 30 minutes. Drain, rinse, discard stems, squeeze out excess moisture, and pat dry.

Cook potatoes in boiling water until tender but still firm. Drain and peel. Cut them into 1/2-inch pieces.

Melt butter and oil together in a large heavy skillet over moderate heat. Sauté shallots and garlic a minute or two and add potatoes.

Sauté together until potatoes are hot and golden. Season with salt and pepper to taste.

Remove potatoes to a heated serving dish and sprinkle with chives and parsley. Serve immediately.

AFTERTHOUGHTS: If you can't find cèpes, try substituting shiitake mushrooms, prepared as above. They are available in Oriental food and grocery stores.

Try adding 1/4 cup minced Westphalian ham or prosciutto with the potatoes.

NANA'S LACY POTATO PANCAKES

8 medium pancakes

Nana serves these crisp, lacy cakes with coarse, freshly cooked applesauce and a fragrant chèvre.

Small handful of parsley leaves
4 large shallots, quartered
2 medium potatoes, unpeeled and
* cut into eighths*
Salt to taste

1 heaping tablespoon Wondra
* flour*
1 egg
Peanut oil for frying

In a food processor, chop parsley and shallots until fine. Add potatoes and continue processing, using on/off pulses until fine but not puréed. Watch carefully.

Add salt, flour and egg and process a few seconds until just blended.

Heat 1/4 inch of peanut oil in a large, heavy skillet. Using 1/4 cup of mixture for each pancake, spread them thinly with the back of a spoon, and fry the cakes until golden and crisp on both sides. Blot them quickly on paper towels and serve immediately.

AFTERTHOUGHT: Without a food processor, simply mince parsley until fine. Grate shallots and potatoes. Combine with remaining ingredients until well blended.

CHAMP IRISH MASHED POTATOES

Serves four to six

They don't get better than this, so there is never enough.

2 pounds white rose or Idaho
  potatoes, peeled and quartered
8 tablespoons butter (or more if
  your diet can take it)
2 bunches scallions, washed,
  trimmed, and chopped

½ cup (or more) milk or
  half-and-half, heated
Salt
Freshly ground black pepper

Boil the potatoes until very tender, drain well, return them to the pan, and shake over the fire a moment or so to dry them thoroughly. (If you can't mash them immediately, cover with a tea towel and keep warm. Don't hold them too long.)

While the potatoes are boiling, melt butter in a small saucepan, add scallions, and sauté slowly until wilted. Do not allow them to brown. Set aside.

Working quickly, mash the potatoes or, better yet, put them through a ricer. Blend in the hot milk, scallions and butter, and salt to taste. Add a grinding or two of pepper and serve very hot.

TIAN OF POTATOES, TOMATOES, AND SCALLIONS

Serves four

Another composition: tender potatoes and rosy tomatoes, laced with scallions and basil. Takes no time at all and is richly rewarding.

3 baking potatoes, scrubbed and
  unpeeled
2 ripe tomatoes
2 bunches scallions, washed and
  trimmed to include 3 inches of
  green tops

⅓ cup olive oil
Salt
Freshly ground black pepper
8–10 fresh basil leaves, torn

Preheat oven to 400°F. Lightly oil a shallow baking dish.

Thinly slice potatoes and tomatoes. Arrange them in overlapping layers in rows in the baking dish. Lay scallions between rows.

Pour olive oil over the vegetables and bake them for 30 to 40 minutes, or until potatoes are tender.

Season to taste with salt and pepper. Scatter basil over the hot vegetables and serve immediately.

AFTERTHOUGHT: Try small yellow squashes, a few mushrooms, crisp green and red peppers—let your tian hold several colors and textures; experiment with fresh herbs. Just remember— thin slices work best.

CHIVE DUMPLINGS, BROWN BUTTER

Serves two

These feathery little dumplings will add a lot of dash to a simple roast chicken. Try them, you'll see.

¾ cup cake flour
¼ cup all-purpose flour
1 teaspoon double-acting baking
  powder
½ teaspoon salt
1 large egg, lightly beaten

2 tablespoons butter, melted and
  cooled
¼ cup sour cream
½ cup minced chives
8 tablespoons unsalted butter

Sift the flours, baking powder, and salt into a medium-size mixing bowl. In a small bowl, beat together the egg, cooled butter, and the sour cream.

Add the egg mixture and chives to the flour and stir until the batter is *just* combined (it is important not to beat this).

With a tablespoon dipped in hot water, drop heaping tablespoons of batter about 2 inches apart onto a buttered, heatproof plate or pie pan. Place the plate on a rack set over simmering water, cover, and steam the dumplings for 10 minutes.

While the dumplings are steaming, heat the 8 tablespoons butter in a small saucepan over moderate heat, swirling the pan, until it is a deep golden brown. Transfer the dumplings to a heated serving plate and pour the butter over them.

BRAISED SCALLIONS

Serves four

Bright scallions are always at their best, so when the other vegetables look droopy and tired, take some scallions home and do this to them—they will always come through for you.

¼ cup water	¼ cup dry vermouth
3 tablespoons butter	Splash of balsamic vinegar
2 bunches scallions, washed and	Salt
trimmed	Freshly ground black pepper

Put water and 2 tablespoons of the butter in a skillet or sauté pan. Bring to a boil and add scallions. Cook about 5 minutes over high heat until water evaporates to about 2 tablespoons. Watch carefully so water does not evaporate completely and scallions burn. Shake pan occasionally.

Add remaining butter and cook over moderate heat until scallions are lightly browned and tender. Remove them to a heated platter and keep warm.

Deglaze the pan with vermouth and vinegar and reduce slightly. Pour over scallions and season with salt and pepper to taste. Serve immediately.

JAPANESE BRAISED SCALLIONS

Serves four

¼ cup water	1 tablespoon Japanese rice
2 tablespoons peanut oil	vinegar
2 bunches of scallions, washed,	3 tablespoons soy sauce
trimmed, and sliced diagonally	1 teaspoon sesame oil
into 3-inch lengths	

Put water and oil in a skillet. Bring to a boil and add scallions. Cook over high heat until water evaporates to about 1 tablespoon, stirring frequently. Do not let scallions burn.

Add rice vinegar and cook over low-moderate heat until scallions are just tender. Add soy sauce and sesame oil and stir to blend. Transfer to a serving dish.

🌿

PEAS WITH SCALLIONS

Serves six

A lively dish; the mint is the kicker. You may substitute a comparable amount of halved, thin-sliced sweet onions or even leeks for the scallions.

1 bunch scallions, washed, trimmed, and cut into ½-inch diagonal slices
4 tablespoons butter
2 packages (10 ounces each) frozen tiny peas, thawed and drained

¼ cup minced fresh mint leaves (failing that, 1 tablespoon crumbled dry mint)
Salt
Freshly ground black pepper

In a large skillet, cook the scallions in the butter, tossing them about now and then over moderate heat until they are suitably softened. Don't brown them.

Add the peas, mint, salt and pepper to taste, and stir together. Cook just until the peas are heated through and the scallions still have their color—and there you are.

AFTERTHOUGHTS: A 1-pound package of tiny pearl onions, defrosted and well drained, may be substituted for the scallions.

Now that I think of it, you could throw the potful of cooked onions and peas into the food processor, purée it, and heat it with a couple of cups of good chicken broth and a cup of cream, and have a great little soup; float a leaf of mint serenely on top of each serving.

✺

SUNDAY SCALLION CAKES

Serves four, and a couple of seconds

My father loved to cook. He approached his forays into the kitchen with enormous enthusiasm, convinced in advance that something terrific was about to be created. Totally free-style and uninhibited, he never looked at a cookbook or a recipe. He just jumped right in and cooked what he wanted just the way he wanted it.

One of his specialties was Sunday breakfast; and how we loved it when he rassled up a monster, down-home morning feast. As his aide-de-camp on these occasions, I was privileged to watch his kitchen performance (offering advice and counsel, which he usually ignored) as he ran up a batch of big, flaky biscuits, thin slices of country ham fried just until the edges frizzled, red-eye gravy that he drizzled over the tops of poached eggs nestled on crisp brown scallion cakes, and all ornamented with sprigs of peppery watercress to drag through the gravy. Sweet butter and clover comb honey accompanied the biscuits. This, of course, all took place in those halcyon days before anyone ever heard of calories, and diets were unknown except as possible aberrations.

And that's Sunday morning for me to this day.

1 *big bunch of scallions, washed, trimmed, and sliced thin*	*Dash of nutmeg*
	Salt
4 *tablespoons butter*	*Freshly ground black pepper*
2 *cups mashed potatoes, cold or hot*	*Cream*
	Flour
1 *egg, lightly beaten*	*Butter or oil for frying*

Toss the sliced scallions around in the butter over medium-low heat until they are softened. Scrape them into the potatoes and mix well.

Blend in the egg, nutmeg, and salt and pepper to taste. Add a little cream or a dollop of yogurt if it seems a little stiff, but take care not to let this stuff get too wet. Taste for seasonings. More pepper, maybe?

Form into 6 patties about 1/2 inch thick. Sprinkle both sides of each one with a little flour and sauté in hot butter until evenly crisp and golden. Add more butter or oil to the skillet as needed.

Remove the cakes to heated plates. You may want to use a kitchen spoon to press an indentation in each one—as a nest for poached eggs, perhaps?

🌺

GRILLED SCALLIONS

There isn't any way to be ladylike about eating these. This is the deal: Buy the smallest ones you can find. When they are properly grilled, blackened here and there and softened, pick one up in your fingers, give it a squirt of lime juice, and pop it into your mouth all at once—yep, all at once. That's the only way to go about it.

I usually allow one bunch per person, and it's barely enough.

6–8 slender scallions per person	*Salt*
(or more!)	*Freshly ground black pepper*
Mild-tasting vegetable oil	*Lime wedges*

Wash scallions carefully. Shake off excess water. Discard unattractive outer leaves and trim ragged tops, but leave roots intact.

Pour a bit of oil in your palm and rub hands together. Lightly oil scallions in your hands. Season to taste with salt and pepper.

Roast them on a grill set over hot coals, turning them as they brown. Watch carefully so they don't burn.

Transfer them to a heated serving plate or scatter them around grilled meats or chicken. Serve with wedges of fresh lime.

AFTERTHOUGHT: You guessed it—this also works beautifully with slender young leeks.

🌺

GOLDEN RICE

Serves four to six

Fragrant with spice and gilded with saffron, this pretty dish is wonderful with curries or any of the oniony ragouts.

2 tablespoons butter
1 cup raw long-grain white rice
2 tablespoons minced scallions,
   white part only
2 cups boiling chicken broth or
   water
Piece of cinnamon stick, about 2
   inches long

½ teaspoon turmeric
Pinch of crumbled saffron
   threads or ground saffron
1 teaspoon salt
½ cup golden raisins
Sugar (optional)
1 teaspoon finely grated lemon
   peel

In a heavy medium saucepan, melt the butter over moderate heat. When it foams, add the rice and scallions and stir until all the grains are coated with butter. Don't let it brown.

Add the broth, cinnamon, turmeric, saffron, and salt. Stirring constantly, bring to a boil over high heat. Reduce heat to low, cover tightly, and simmer 20 minutes, or until the rice is tender and the liquid is absorbed. Remove from heat.

Discard the cinnamon stick and add the raisins. Taste for seasoning; add a bit of sugar if you like. Fluff ingredients together and place a circle of foil or kitchen parchment directly on the rice. Cover the pan and let it rest at room temperature for 20 minutes. Just before serving, fluff the rice again and mound it prettily on a heated serving dish. Sprinkle the lemon peel on top.

SPINACH AND SCALLION SAUTÉ

Boy, is this good!

3 tablespoons peanut oil
1 garlic clove, peeled and bruised
1 teaspoon minced fresh ginger
1 green chili, minced
1 pound spinach, well washed
   and dried, tough stems
   removed, and coarsely chopped

1 bunch scallions, cut in 2-inch
   julienne
½ teaspoon sugar
Salt

In a large skillet or wok, heat oil over moderate to high heat. Toss in garlic and stir-fry for 30 seconds; discard garlic.

Add ginger and chili and stir-fry 30 to 45 seconds. Add spinach and scallions and sprinkle with sugar and salt to taste. Sauté until wilted, 1 to 2 minutes. Serve immediately, or chill and serve with a sprinkling of toasted sesame seeds and Japanese salad vinegar.

❧

LENTILS WITH SHALLOTS AND CHILIES

Serves four to six

To tell you the truth, I never thought about lentils one way or another until I lucked into this North African way with them. As I am unable to stick to any recipe, I added fresh lemon juice and garnished the lentils with a handful of brilliant calendula and geranium petals that happened to be drying (potential potpourri) in my kitchen that day. It was very festive and had a subtle, smoky flavor, zingy with chilies and shallots. My friends ate every bit of it and wrote the recipe on scraps of paper for future reference—now that's a reference!

A word of advice: The small serrano chilies called for in this recipe can be torrid and, if you're not all that nuts about hot stuff, you can substitute the long green Anaheim variety; they are somewhat milder. If you use the fresh ones, they add a nice crunch. If you do use them, don't bother to roast and peel them, just seed them and cut into nice long strips.

Lentils, by the way, are full of high-powered protein, minerals and such, and they are good for you.

*1¼ cups (½ pound) dried
lentils, washed and drained
6 garlic cloves, peeled
Salt
3 tablespoons red wine vinegar
2 tablespoons mild vegetable oil
Freshly ground black pepper*

*8 large shallots, sliced into
quarters
2 fresh hot green serrano chilies,
about 3 inches long, stemmed,
seeded, and cut into 1½-inch
long thin strips*

Place lentils in a medium saucepan and pour enough water over them to cover by 2 inches. Add garlic cloves and salt to taste and bring to a boil. Reduce heat to low, partly cover, and simmer 30 minutes, or until lentils are tender but firm. Drain.

Whisk the vinegar, oil, 1 teaspoon salt, and pepper together in a deep bowl. Add the lentils, shallots, and chilies and blend well. Taste for seasoning. Let lentils marinate at room temperature for at least 1 hour, stirring occasionally. Serve them mounded attractively on a small platter.

SLAM-BANG BEANS

Serves eight to ten

Everybody knows that good beans are central to a barbecue, and this bean concoction packs a real wallop. You can get them ready a day or two in advance and leave them to their own devices in the refrigerator to mellow. Heat them on the stove, or let them simmer away in the oven for an hour or two where they will take on a lovely glaze while you give your attention to other matters—like directing kitchen traffic.

Life is a beautiful thing, so round up your pals and celebrate the summer; it's later than you think!

2 pounds dried pinto or red beans (or 12 cups canned beans, if the moment is desperate)
2 onions, halved
3 garlic cloves
¼ cup peanut oil
4 cups chopped onion
10 garlic cloves, crushed
2 green peppers, cored, seeded, and chopped
1 pound bulk sausage
2 pounds pork butt, cut into thin strips
6 ripe tomatoes, chopped

1 tablespoon dried oregano
3 tablespoons chili powder
1 tablespoon cumin seeds, toasted and crushed
1 teaspoon minced fresh ginger
¾ cup dark brown sugar
¼ cup molasses
1 large can crushed tomatoes
½ cup red wine vinegar
2–3 jalapeño peppers, finely chopped
Salt
Freshly ground black pepper
Crushed dried red chilies to taste

Cook beans according to package directions, i.e. soak overnight with water to cover, etc., but add a couple of onions, halved, and several garlic cloves to the cooking water. Remove the onions after cooking. Drain the beans, but reserve the liquid in case you need some later to add to the pot.

Heat oil in a very large heavy casserole. Add onions, garlic, and green pepper, and cook over low heat, covered, until the onions are tender and translucent, about 10 minutes.

Crumble sausage meat into the pot and add the pork strips. Cook over medium-high heat, stirring often, until meats are brown. Spoon out as much fat as possible.

Add remaining ingredients and reserved beans and combine. Simmer in a slow (325°F) oven, or over *low* heat on the back of the stove, at least 1 hour, or until needed. Add reserved bean liquid if things look a bit dry. At some time during the simmering, taste for seasonings and adjust. Serve with barbecued ribs and chicken and mugs of severely cold beer.

SALADS AND DRESSINGS

MONTEREY CHICKEN SALAD

Serves four

A lively update of an old favorite—and full of surprises. It's gorgeous!

2 heads butter lettuce, washed,
dried, tough outer leaves
discarded, and torn
1 bunch watercress, washed,
dried, leaves only
½ cup flour
Salt
Freshly ground black pepper
⅓ cup milk
½ cup peanut oil
2 whole chicken breasts, halved,
skinned and boned, and sliced
into ½-inch-wide strips
1 tablespoon balsamic vinegar
1 tablespoon apple cider vinegar

2 teaspoons Dijon mustard
1 large shallot, minced
1 tablespoon chopped fresh
tarragon leaves, or 1 teaspoon
dried
1 tablespoon capers, drained
(optional)
1 medium sweet red Italian
onion, thinly sliced
1 large sweet red pepper, cored,
seeded, and cut into julienne
1 small jicama, peeled and cut
into julienne
Minced chives

Arrange lettuce and watercress leaves in a large shallow serving bowl.

Combine flour and salt and pepper to taste in a bowl. Pour milk into another bowl.

Heat peanut oil in a heavy skillet over moderately high heat.

Dip chicken strips into milk and then into flour mixture. Fry strips in hot oil until golden brown, about 5 minutes. Drain on paper towels. Reserve oil in pan off heat.

Combine vinegars, mustard, and shallot in a mixing bowl. Pour in reserved oil and beat vigorously with a wire whisk. Season to taste with salt and pepper. Blend in tarragon leaves and capers.

Mound chicken in center of lettuce and arrange onion slices, pepper strips, and jicama attractively on platter. Combine dressing once more and either pour over salad just before presenting the salad or at the table. Toss to moisten and serve immediately, garnished with chives.

AFTERTHOUGHTS: This becomes Oriental Chicken Salad with the addition of Chinese peas, toasted sesame seeds, water chestnuts in lieu of jicama, and julienne scallions in place of onion slices. Toss with a warm dressing of oil, rice wine vinegar, hoisin sauce (from Oriental markets) and a bit of fresh ginger.

Try substituting barely sautéed scallops for the chicken, or cubes of fried fish (monkfish, halibut, or red snapper would be wonderful).

Or substitute strips of Chinese roast pork and fresh pineapple for the chicken. Wow!

❦

GADO GADO SALAD

Serves four

A lavish salad with an exotic dressing.

THE SAUCE

½ cup finely chopped onion
1 garlic clove, minced
1 or 2 thin slices fresh ginger, peeled and minced
1 fresh green chili, seeded and finely chopped
3 tablespoons vegetable oil
1 tablespoon brown sugar (or to taste)
1 teaspoon chili powder
Juice of 1 lime
¼ cup coconut milk, frozen or canned
½ cup crunchy peanut butter
¼ cup torn cilantro leaves
Salt
Freshly ground black pepper

THE SALAD

Shredded iceberg lettuce
1 cup shredded cold roast chicken
1 cup julienned Chinese roast pork or medium whole cooked shrimp

1 cup string beans, parboiled crisp-tender, drained, and left whole
1 cup julienned carrots, parboiled crisp-tender, drained
1 cup blanched cabbage or bok choy, drained and shredded
4 hard-boiled eggs, quartered
1 small cucumber, peeled, halved lengthwise, seeded, and cut into ¼-inch slices
2 or 3 medium-size ripe tomatoes, sliced into eighths
¼ cup thinly sliced shallots, browned lightly in oil, drained
6 or 8 small radishes, thinly sliced
4 scallions, washed, trimmed, and slivered

Sauté onion, garlic, ginger, and chili in oil until onion becomes transparent. Add sugar and chili powder and cook over low heat 5 minutes, stirring frequently. Stir in lime juice, coconut milk, peanut butter, and cilantro leaves and remove from heat. Season to taste with salt and pepper. Spoon into small individual serving bowls. Set aside.

Cover the bottom of a large serving platter with shredded lettuce. Mound the two meats decoratively in the center and surround them in a spoke-like pattern with the string beans, carrots, cabbage, eggs, cucumber, and tomato slices. Garnish with shallots, radishes, and scallions. Let your guests help themselves to the salad ingredients, adding as much gado gado sauce as they wish. Have chopped green chilies, lime wedges, brown sugar, salt, and pepper available so you may season sauce to taste.

AFTERTHOUGHT: The gado gado sauce would be marvelous served on paillard of chicken. Or for a touch of the mysterious East serve it with skewered meats or chicken. (Thread some cubes of lamb with lemon slices and quartered onions, brush with a mixture of lemon juice and oil, barbecue them, and serve with gado gado and Japanese white rice).

Spoon gado gado over quarters of steamed cabbage. It's real good.

MOROCCAN SALAD

Serves six

The gentle sweetness of the oranges is just the thing to serve with any dishes that are hot and spicy.

12–14 young radishes, about 1 bunch
6 scallions, minced, green and all
4 large navel oranges, peel and pith discarded, cut into chunks
¼ cup fresh lemon juice

2 tablespoons sugar (or to taste)
2 tablespoons olive oil
1 teaspoon cumin seeds, toasted and crushed
Coarsely ground black pepper to taste
Red leaf lettuce

Chop the radishes coarsely and squeeze out excess juice in paper towels.

Toss everything together but the cumin, pepper, and lettuce.

To serve, arrange the salad on a bed of red leaf lettuce. Sprinkle with toasted cumin and a grinding of pepper.

AFTERTHOUGHT: You may make this salad a day in advance. Keep it refrigerated and covered.

MUSSELS AND RED POTATOES, VINAIGRETTE

Serves six

Sturdy and reliable, a warm salad that needs nothing but something crisp and raw to nibble on while you put it all together, a full-bodied young red wine or icy beer—and a wicked dessert.

4 pounds mussels (New Zealands are the best)
1½ cups white wine
3–4 garlic cloves, peeled and chopped
½ cup chopped shallots or scallions
1 bay leaf
½ teaspoon dried thyme
3 pounds small red potatoes, unpeeled
½ cup olive oil

¼ cup sherry wine vinegar
1 tablespoon finely diced sweet red pepper
1 shallot, minced
1 teaspoon Dijon mustard
½ cup thinly sliced scallions, including green tops
Salt
Freshly ground black pepper
Red cabbage or radicchio leaves
¼ cup minced parsley

Clean and debeard mussels. Soak for 1 hour in cold water.

Bring wine, garlic, chopped shallots, bay leaf, and thyme to a boil in a large saucepan with a cup of water. Lower heat and simmer. Add mussels and cook gently 6 or 7 minutes, or until they are all opened. Remove mussels and set aside. Strain and reserve 3/4 cup of mussel broth.

Cook potatoes in a large pot of boiling water until just tender.

Drain and cut into 1/4-inch slices while they are still warm, but do not peel.

Combine olive oil, vinegar, diced pepper, reserved mussel broth, minced shallot, and mustard in a small bowl.

Heat the vinaigrette to simmering and pour over the warm potatoes. Add sliced scallions and mussels, and season to taste with salt and pepper. Place each serving on a leaf of red cabbage or radicchio, garnish with parsley, and serve at room temperature.

CALIFORNIA SHRIMP SALAD

Serves six

Just possibly one of the finest things to happen to shrimps in a very long time. Luxurious and as simple as can be.

5 perfectly ripe small avocados
Juice of 2 limes
5 large shallots, finely chopped
2 pounds large green (raw) shrimp, or 1 pound large cooked shrimp

Fruity olive oil
Salt
Freshly cracked black pepper
½ bunch cilantro leaves, torn
1 small bunch chives, snipped

Peel, pit, and cut avocados into 1-inch chunks. Combine them in a large serving bowl with the lime juice and shallots, tossing gently. (You may want to use more lime juice.)

Peel the shrimp and drop them in boiling water until just pink, a minute or two. Do not overcook them as they lose their delicate, crisp texture and turn hard. Remove them immediately. As soon as they are cool enough to handle, peel and remove veins. Slice each shrimp into thirds and add them to the avocados.

Drizzle with enough olive oil to dress, not drown, the salad, and season with salt and pepper. Sprinkle on the cilantro and chives and toss again. Serve immediately.

MIXED GREEN SALAD WITH SURPRISES

Serves six

The title says it all.

Handful of young spinach leaves,
  torn
1 bunch watercress leaves
1 head butter lettuce leaves, torn
Inner leaves of 1 large heart of
  romaine, torn
6 ounces white Cheddar cheese,
  coarsely grated

¾ cup coarsely chopped walnuts,
  toasted in 1 tablespoon walnut
  or peanut oil and cooled
Shallot Vinaigrette (recipe
  follows)

Combine greens, Cheddar, and walnuts in a large salad bowl. Drizzle with enough Shallot Vinaigrette to dress the salad and mix together with a light hand.

AFTERTHOUGHT: A cored, sliced red pear (unpeeled) is *very* good in this salad.

SHALLOT VINAIGRETTE

About 3/4 cup

½ cup fresh parsley sprigs
2 large shallots
2 tablespoons red wine vinegar
4 teaspoons Dijon mustard
1 teaspoon sugar

½ teaspoon salt
Freshly ground black pepper
⅔ cup peanut oil
3 tablespoons olive oil

Place the parsley, shallots, and vinegar in a blender and give them a few whirls to mince the parsley and shallots. Add the mustard, sugar, salt, and pepper and spin again.

With the motor running, add the oils in a thin stream. Store in a covered container in the refrigerator.

COLD LEEKS IN MUSTARD SAUCE

Serves six

What a nice dish for a summer luncheon.

12 leeks, about 1 inch thick,
   well washed and trimmed of
   all but 1 inch of green top
2 tablespoons butter
Salt
Freshly ground black pepper
2 eggs
2 teaspoons Dijon mustard
2 teaspoons sherry wine vinegar
1 cup peanut oil
½ cup minced parsley
2 teaspoons dried dillweed
2 tablespoons minced scallion
12 thin slices prosciutto
6 whole radishes
Watercress sprigs

Place leeks in a single layer in a large skillet and cover with water by 1 inch. Add butter and salt and pepper to taste. Bring to a boil over high heat and simmer for 8 to 10 minutes, or until leeks are tender when pierced with the tip of a sharp knife. Drain on paper towels and set aside.

In a blender or food processor, combine the eggs, mustard, vinegar, and salt and pepper to taste. Whirl until well combined. With the machine running, add the oil drop by drop until the sauce is thick and smooth. Taste and adjust seasonings. Add parsley, dill, and scallion, and whirl until combined.

Wrap each leek in a slice of prosciutto and arrange in a single layer on a serving plate. Spoon the sauce over, completely covering the leeks. Garnish with the radishes and sprigs of watercress.

AFTERTHOUGHT: Sauce may be made in advance and refrigerated overnight.

LEEKS À LA GRECQUE

Serves three to four

Leeks can sing this song alone or in concert with tiny onions, artichoke hearts, celery, mushrooms, or sliced fennel. Add some olives and a few chopped ripe tomatoes (don't cook these). Feel free to make up your own chorus.

½ cup fruity olive oil
1 cup water
1 small garlic clove, unpeeled,
  crushed
Juice of 2 small lemons
Slice or two of lemon peel
1 teaspoon dried tarragon
½ teaspoon dried thyme

3 parsley sprigs
Salt
Freshly ground black pepper
8 medium leeks, white part only,
  well washed, trimmed, and
  cut into 1½-inch diagonal
  slices

In a glass or stainless-steel saucepan, combine everything but the leeks. Bring to a boil, reduce heat, and simmer for 15 minutes.

Add the prepared leeks to the simmering marinade and cook until just crisp-tender, about 10 minutes.

Allow the leeks to cool in the marinade. Serve as an appetizer.

AFTERTHOUGHTS: You may prepare vegetables in this manner a day or two in advance. Keep refrigerated, but allow them to stand at room temperature 30 minutes before you serve them.

Different vegetables require varying cooking times. Small onions, for instance, may take 20 to 30 minutes until tender, mushroom only 3 or 4.

The marinade is also delicious with the addition of fennel seeds, oregano, dried coriander, or dill seeds. Try your favorites. And experiment with vegetables, too.

WARM LEEK AND POTATO SALAD

Serves four to six

A jug of wine, this salad, some Basque chicken sandwiches, fresh ripe fruit, and thou.

6 medium red potatoes, unpeeled
6 slender leeks (thumb-size, if
  possible), well washed
2 tablespoons best olive oil
1 small jar marinated artichoke
  hearts
1 small sweet red pepper, cored,
  seeded, and cut into julienne
½ cup frozen tiny green peas,
  defrosted

Salt
Freshly ground black pepper
Shallot Vinaigrette (page 211)
4 hard-boiled eggs, peeled and
  quartered
Snipped fresh chives
Minced fresh parsley

Boil the potatoes until tender, but still firm. Drain. When cool enough to handle, slice them and keep warm.

Trim the leeks, leaving 1 1/2 to 2 inches of green tops, and slice them into 1-inch diagonals. Sauté them in olive oil until just crisp-tender.

In a glass salad bowl, combine the warm potatoes and leeks, the artichokes and their marinade, red pepper, and peas. Season with salt and a grinding or two of pepper.

Dress the salad with enough Shallot Vinaigrette to moisten and toss gently. Garnish with quartered eggs and sprinkle with chives and parsley. Serve warm.

WELSH LEEK SALAD

Serves four

When the Welsh are not wearing their prized leeks in their hatbands, they sometimes make this salad with them. You can, too.

12 small leeks (about the size of
  your thumb)
Chicken broth to cover
¾ cup olive oil
¼ cup red wine vinegar
Salt
Freshly ground black pepper

1 tablespoon grated onion
1 tablespoon each chopped fresh
  parsley and chives
2 teaspoons capers, coarsely
  chopped
1 hard-boiled egg, chopped

Wash leeks thoroughly. Trim roots and tops, leaving only 2 inches of green. Simmer them in chicken broth until tender. Do not over-cook. Drain and dry the leeks, and place them on a serving plate. (Save broth for another use).

In a small saucepan, combine and heat the olive oil, vinegar, salt, pepper, and grated onion. Do not allow the mixture to boil.

Remove the oil mixture from the heat and add the parsley, chives, capers, and chopped egg, stirring well. Pour over the leeks and allow them to marinate for an hour or two. Serve at room temperature.

AFTERTHOUGHT: You'll also enjoy this made with whole slender scallions. Leave 3 or 4 inches of their green tops.

MARIA ELENA'S ENSALADA PICANTE

Serves four to six

Maria Elena garnishes her chicken soup with this salad; I like to serve it along with Slam-Bang Beans (page 204).

1 bunch scallions, washed, trimmed, and finely chopped
1 cucumber, peeled, seeded, and chopped
3 cups chopped cabbage
6–8 radishes, chopped
2 large ripe tomatoes, halved, seeded, and chopped
1 large avocado, diced
1–2 fresh green chilies, seeded, and minced

½ teaspoon cumin seeds, roasted and crushed
½ teaspoon dried oregano
Mild-tasting vegetable oil
Red wine vinegar
Salt
Freshly ground black pepper
Squeeze of lemon or lime juice

In a large bowl combine scallions, cucumber, cabbage, radishes, tomatoes, avocado, and chilies. Spoon cumin and oregano into the palm of your hand and, rubbing palms together, sprinkle them over the vegetables.

Drizzle with oil just to coat ingredients, and toss. Sprinkle with vinegar to taste and toss again. Season with salt and a few grindings of pepper. Now toss everything together a third time and taste. Not enough vinegar? Add some. Needs more oregano? Ditto. Maria Elena says this is the fun part of salad making. Tasting and tossing. When it's just about right, add the squeeze of lemon or lime. "Now it's perfect!"

SAUCES

BEURRE BLANC

1 1/2 cups

The empress of sauces, unchallenged for its richness. It is divine with veal, fish, poached eggs, chicken dishes, and vegetables.

1 cup dry white wine   *¾ pound unsalted butter*
2 shallots, chopped   *Juice of ½ lemon*
1 tablespoon chopped tarragon   *½ teaspoon salt*
½ cup whipping cream   *¼ teaspoon white pepper*

In a medium saucepan, combine wine, shallots, and tarragon. Reduce liquid over moderately high heat until approximately 1/3 cup remains.

Add cream and continue to reduce to 1/2 cup.

Lower heat and whisk butter into mixture, 2 tablespoons at a time. Be careful that the mixture doesn't boil or get too cold; keep temperature constant.

Add remaining ingredients. Taste and adjust seasonings. Strain and serve.

AFTERTHOUGHT: Prepare only as much as you think you will need. Beurre blanc separates when reheated.

BEURRE ROUGE

1 cup

Spoon this over grilled meats, fish, or poached eggs.

2 shallots, finely minced
½ teaspoon finely minced parsley
⅓ cup red Burgundy wine
2 tablespoons red wine vinegar
½ pound chilled unsalted butter,
*   cut into small pieces*

1 tablespoon whipping cream
Salt
Freshly ground black pepper

Boil the shallots, parsley, wine, and vinegar together in a 1 1/2-quart porcelain or stainless steel saucepan, until reduced to about 1 1/2 tablespoons.

Remove saucepan from the heat. Immediately beat in 2 pieces of chilled butter. As the butter creams into the liquid, beat in another piece. Place the saucepan over *very* low heat and, whisking constantly, continue adding butter a piece at a time, incorporating each piece before adding another. Do not let mixture boil or get too cold. The sauce will be thick, the consistency of light hollandaise.

Immediately remove from the heat as soon as all butter has been added. Beat in cream and season to taste with salt and pepper. Serve immediately.

SAUCE BERCY

About 1/2 cup

Sauce Bercy is simple to make and very French. It goes well with many, many dishes: eggs, steak, fish, and calf's liver, and it gives a broiled hamburger a whole new dimension.

4 medium shallots, minced
1 cup full-bodied red wine
4 tablespoons butter
Few drops lemon

Salt
Freshly ground black pepper
1 teaspoon minced parsley

Simmer the shallots and wine together until the wine is reduced to 1/4 cup.

Over low heat whisk in the butter a teaspoon at a time. Don't bother to measure the butter, just take it in your hand and pinch it off into the simmering wine mixture, shaking the pan with your other hand. As soon as one lump is absorbed, squeeze in another and keep shaking the pan. Don't fiddle around with this step; just do it.

When all the butter is absorbed, stir in the lemon juice, salt, pepper, and parsley. Do not allow the sauce to boil. Serve hot.

MUSTARD SHALLOT SAUCE

About 1 1/4 cups

For fish, shellfish, and extra good on grilled chicken.

1 cup dry white wine
3 large shallots, chopped
1 tablespoon fresh tarragon leaves, chopped
4 tablespoons whipping cream
½ pound unsalted butter

1 tablespoon Dijon mustard
2 tablespoons minced chives
Salt
Freshly ground black pepper
Juice of ½ lemon

In a small saucepan, combine the wine, shallots, and tarragon. Reduce over moderate heat until 2 tablespoons remain.

Add cream and reduce once more to 2 tablespoons.

Slowly add the butter, about a tablespoon at a time, whisking all the while. Do not boil. Strain. Stir in the mustard and chives. Add salt, pepper, and lemon juice to taste. Serve immediately.

TOMATO, SHALLOT, AND CAPER SAUCE

1 cup

Provençal to the bone, a fine sauce spooned over cold poached fish, sliced cold meats, scrambled eggs, or what you will.

2–3 *large shallots, minced*
1 *hard-boiled egg, mashed*
2 *tablespoons finely chopped*
parsley
½ *cup cored, halved, seeded, and*
finely chopped ripe tomatoes

3 *tablespoons red wine vinegar*
⅓ *cup finest olive oil*
1 *tablespoon capers, drained*
Salt
Freshly ground black pepper

Combine shallots, egg, parsley, tomatoes, and vinegar in a small bowl.

Whisk in olive oil a spoonful at a time.

Stir in capers. Season to taste with salt and pepper, and serve at room temperature.

SHALLOT BUTTER SAUCE

1/2 cup

An excellent sauce for London broil, or when you lack pan juices.

8 *tablespoons unsalted butter*
6–8 *large shallots, chopped fine*
Pinch of salt

Grinding or two of black pepper
Dash of cayenne

Heat butter in a deep saucepan until it is *just* beginning to brown. Remove pan from heat and drop in shallots. Swirl them around in the butter (away from your face—they will bubble up).

Season with salt and pepper to taste, and a bit of cayenne.

AFTERTHOUGHT: A tablespoon of dry red wine would be a nice touch.

After sautéing meat or chicken, pour off all but a tablespoon of fat, add a couple of tablespoons of minced shallots and sauté for 1 minute. Pour in a little beef broth (canned is fine), a splash of dry vermouth, wine, or cognac, and cook until sauce reduces and thickens. Sprinkle with chopped parsley or chives and spoon over the meat. Don't forget the salt and pepper.

❧

SPRINGTIME SAUCE

About 3/4 cup

This sauce is splendid with poached, grilled, sautéed, or baked fish; paillard of chicken; steamed vegetables.

1 ripe tomato, peeled, seeded,
  and diced
¼ teaspoon crushed coriander
  seed
Juice of 1 lemon
½ cup olive oil

Salt
Freshly ground black pepper
1 tablespoon fresh tarragon,
  chervil or basil, minced, or a
  combination
¼ cup minced chives

Combine tomato, coriander, and lemon juice in a blender. With motor running, add oil a few drops at a time until thickened and emulsified.

Season to taste with salt and pepper. Turn out into a small serving dish. Add herbs and combine gently, saving a sprinkling for garnish.

❧

CHIVE SABAYON SAUCE FOR FISH

About 1 cup

This lovely sauce, light in calories, is just right for delicate fish.

1–2 bay leaves
Handful of parsley
Leaves from 2 stalks of celery
⅔ cup boiling chicken broth
  (no fat)

3 egg yolks
1 tablespoon fresh lemon juice
3 tablespoons snipped chives
Salt

Place the bay leaves, parsley, and celery leaves in a small bowl. Pour the boiling broth over them and allow the leaves to steep until cool.

Half fill the bottom of a double boiler with hot water and and put the egg yolks in the top. Strain the cooled broth and add to the eggs.

Whisk over moderate heat until the egg yolks foam and thicken and a light sauce forms, taking care not to let the heat get too high or the eggs will curdle. Whisk in the lemon juice, chives, and a dash of salt. Serve at once.

AFTERTHOUGHT: This sauce will hold for a half an hour or so in the top of the double boiler over low heat. Whisk up again just before serving.

SCALLION SAUCE

2 cups

Maybe the title isn't lyrical, but the sauce is! Try it over steamed vegetables, grilled, fried, or poached fish or shrimp.

2 teaspoons cornstarch
1 cup chicken broth
1 tablespoon sugar
⅓ cup soy sauce
⅓ cup dry sherry
1 tablespoon wine vinegar
½ sweet red pepper, cored, seeded, and cut into julienne

2 teaspoons grated fresh ginger
2 garlic cloves, minced
2 tablespoons peanut oil
1 cup thinly sliced scallions, including green tops
2 tablespoons toasted sesame seeds

In a bowl, dissolve the cornstarch in 1/4 cup of the broth. Add sugar, remaining broth, soy sauce, sherry, and vinegar; stir well.

Sauté the pepper, ginger, and garlic in peanut oil just until they soften. Do not allow them to brown.

Stir seasoned broth once more and add to pepper and ginger. Simmer over moderate heat until the sauce is clear and shiny.

Add scallions and allow them to just heat through. Serve at once garnished with sesame seeds.

SCALLION AND CUCUMBER SAUCE

About 1 1/2 cups

A light fresh sauce that is delicious on steamed or broiled fish.

1 tablespoon unsalted butter
6–8 slender scallions, washed,
trimmed, and thinly sliced on
the diagonal
1 cucumber, peeled, seeded, and
diced (not too fine)

⅓ cup cream
1 teaspoon dried dillweed
⅓ cup sour cream
Salt
Freshly ground black pepper
Lemon juice to taste

Melt the butter in a small saucepan and cook the scallions and diced cucumber over low heat until the cucumber is softened and the scallions are bright green.

Add the cream and dill and simmer for a few minutes until the cream is slightly reduced.

Add sour cream, salt, and pepper. Taste for seasoning; give it a hit of lemon juice just for kicks. Simmer for a few minutes, but don't let it boil.

BREADS

HERBED FOCACCIA

Serves six as hors d'oeuvres, or
two to three at lunch

It's clear that there are about a hundred ways to play around with this dough—have some fun with it. Focaccia is great cut up in small squares and served warm with drinks, or soup, or . . .

1 package active dry yeast
1 cup lukewarm water
Pinch of sugar
1½ cups all-purpose flour
Salt
4 tablespoons olive oil
1 medium onion, thinly sliced
1 garlic clove, minced

1 teaspoon herbes de Provence, or
dried oregano, thyme, or
marjoram, or a mixture
Freshly ground black pepper
Cornmeal
½ cup grated Monterey jack,
mild Cheddar, mozzarella,
and/or Parmesan cheese

Combine yeast, warm water, and sugar in a large bowl. Let stand until foamy, about 5 minutes. Mix in 1 cup of the flour and 1/2 teaspoon salt. Add enough remaining flour to form a dough that pulls away from the sides of the bowl. Turn dough out onto a lightly floured surface and knead until smooth and elastic, about 5 minutes.

Place the dough ball in a warm, oiled bowl, turning dough to coat with oil. Cover and let rise in a warm spot in the kitchen until doubled in size, about 1 hour.

Meanwhile, heat 2 tablespoons of the oil in a heavy skillet over low heat. Add onion and sauté until barely tender, about 20 minutes, adding garlic and herbs for the last 5 minutes of cooking. Season with salt and pepper. Remove from heat.

Punch down dough and turn it out onto a lightly floured surface. Roll into a 1/2-inch-thick rectangle. Transfer to a cookie sheet that has been sprinkled with cornmeal. Allow to rise another 20 minutes.

Using your first two fingers, make indentations over the surface of dough. Spread with onion mixture and sprinkle with cheese. Drizzle with remaining olive oil and let rise another 20 to 30 minutes.

Preheat oven to 425°F.

Bake bread until crisp and golden brown, about 25 minutes. Cut into squares and serve warm or cooled.

AFTERTHOUGHT: Use this as the basis for outstanding pizza, topping it with whatever suits your fancy.

MONKEY BREAD WITH SCALLIONS
AND POPPY SEEDS

One loaf

When I make these rolls for the men in my cooking classes, they seldom reach the table—the rolls, that is. These buttery little darlings are usually wolfed down by those ruffians on the way to the dining room.

1 loaf frozen bread dough, defrosted (Bridgeford is excellent)	*1 bunch slender scallions, washed, trimmed and sliced thin*
5 tablespoons butter	*Butter for baking pan*
	3 tablespoons poppy seeds

Follow instructions on bread label, allowing dough to rise in a warm spot until double in size.

Meanwhile, melt butter in a small saucepan over low heat. Add scallions and cook them until slightly softened. Set aside.

Lavishly butter a 10-inch bundt or tube pan. Spoon 2 or 3 tablespoons scallion-butter mixture onto bottom of pan. Sprinkle with one third of the poppy seeds.

Punch down the dough and roll out into a rectangle about 1/2 inch thick. Using a 2- to 2 1/2-inch biscuit cutter or juice glass, cut dough into rounds. Dip each round into butter mixture and arrange half the rounds in an overlapping layer on the bottom of the pan. Spoon another 2 or 3 tablespoons of scallion butter over this layer and sprinkle with a tablespoon of poppy seeds. Repeat procedure with remaining dough, butter mixture, and poppy seeds. (The dough will push its way into the empty spots as it bakes.)

Cover with a tea towel and let rise until nearly doubled. Bake in a preheated 350° oven for 1 hour, or until loaf sounds hollow when tapped. Invert pan onto serving plate and slip out bread. Turn it right side up and serve immediately.

AFTERTHOUGHT: You could make this with your own homemade dough if you wish, but the frozen dough speeds up the process and no one is the wiser.

CHEESE AND SCALLION TOASTS

About 72 triangles

Great with drinks.

2 cups minced scallions,
  including green tops
⅓ cup minced parsley
1 cup grated sharp Cheddar
  cheese
½ cup mayonnaise
1 tablespoon Worcestershire sauce

Dash of Tabasco
36 *thin slices French or Italian*
  bread, crusts removed, and cut
  into 3-inch triangles. The
  yield will vary depending on
  the size of the bread. Save the
  scraps for bread crumbs.

Preheat broiler.

In a small bowl (or perhaps the food processor) combine the scallions, parsley, cheese, mayonnaise, and seasonings.

Place bread triangles on a baking sheet and lightly toast one side under the broiler.

Turn the slices over and spread the scallion mixture on the untoasted side, covering each slice completely (that's all the way out to the edges).

Return the toasts to the broiler for 3 to 5 minutes, or until the scallion mixture is bubbling and golden.

SCALLION TOASTS

25 slices

These toasts are very good in, or with, a bowl of soup.

4 tablespoons butter
⅓ cup olive oil
½ cup minced scallions,
  including green tops

25 *slices French or Italian*
  bread, about ¼ inch thick

Preheat oven to 350°F.

Melt the butter and oil together. Add scallions but do not cook.

Arrange the bread slices on an oiled baking sheet and brush with the butter mixture. Bake in the preheated oven for 20 to 25 minutes, or until golden. Serve warm or at room temperature.

SCALLION AND GREEN CHILI ROLLS

12 rolls

A California special. Here are yeast rolls that won't hang you up all day. They have an interesting flavor, and the cornmeal gives them a nice texture.

¾ cup warm water
1 package active dry yeast
1 teaspoon salt
1 tablespoon sugar
2 tablespoons green chili salsa
  (or more)
1 egg, at room temperature
2 tablespoons butter, softened

1¼ cups all-purpose flour
1 cup cornmeal
1 bunch slender scallions, green
  and all, washed, trimmed,
  and thinly sliced
½ cup grated sharp Cheddar
  cheese

Pour the water into a large bowl and sprinkle the yeast over it, stirring until the yeast dissolves. Let stand 5 minutes.

Stir in salt, sugar, green chili salsa, egg, butter, and 1 cup of the flour; beat until smooth. Add cornmeal, remaining flour, scallions, and cheese. Beat again. Cover and allow to rise until doubled in bulk.

Preheat oven to 400°F.

Butter 12 muffin cups. Stir down the batter and beat about 25 strokes. Spoon into muffin cups and let stand about 20 minutes, or until doubled in size.

Bake rolls 15 minutes, or until lightly browned.

🌿

SCALLION CRÊPES

An accompaniment to many foods.

2 eggs, lightly beaten	*½ teaspoon ground allspice*
½ cup chopped scallions,	*Salt*
including green tops	*Freshly ground black pepper*
½ cup minced parsley	*½ cup peanut oil*
1 teaspoon flour	

Combine eggs, scallions, parsley, flour, and seasonings and mix well.

In a heavy skillet, heat the oil over moderate heat until hot. Drop tablespoons of the scallion mixture 1 1/2 inches apart and cook the crêpes for 45 seconds on each side. Transfer to paper towels to drain. Serve at once.

Odd Bulbs
🌿

SALT-FREE SEASONING

About 2/3 cup

Here's one way to spice up your life without using any salt.

Peel from 3 oranges (no pith)	*1 tablespoon dried sage*
Peel from 3 lemons (no pith)	*1 tablespoon dried marjoram*
¼ pound shallots, sliced paper	*1 tablespoon dried oregano*
thin	*1 teaspoon dried red pepper*
10 large garlic cloves, sliced	*flakes*
paper thin	*1–2 tablespoons freshly ground*
¼ cup dried thyme	*black pepper*
2 tablespoons dried rosemary	*¼ teaspoon cayenne*

Dry orange and lemon peel, shallot, and garlic on a rack or screen at room temperature for 3 or 4 days, or until brittle.

In a blender or food processor, grind all ingredients except cayenne in batches until powdered. Sift through a fine sieve into a large bowl. Add cayenne and blend thoroughly.

Transfer seasoning to an airtight container and store in a cool, dark, dry place.

LEEK WREATHS VINAIGRETTE

A very dressy presentation for hot or cold poached salmon or other fish, or paillard of chicken.

1 medium leek per serving   *Salt*
1 part red wine vinegar   *Freshly ground pepper*
1 part lemon juice
5 or 6 parts peanut or other
  mild-tasting vegetable oil

Trim the roots from the leeks and remove outermost tough leaves. Trim ragged green ends.

Halve the leeks lengthwise, almost cutting through the white root end. Wash well under cold running water. Tie the leeks into bundles with string.

Bring a large pot of water to a boil and drop in leek bundles. Lower heat and simmer them for 10 minutes or so, just until tender. Be careful not to overcook.

Meanwhile, whisk vinegar, lemon juice, and oil together in a small bowl until emulsified. Set aside.

Drain leeks in a colander. Discard strings and press out any excess water with the back of a large spoon. Place leeks on a heated plate and sprinkle with the vinaigrette. Season with salt and pepper to taste and keep warm.

To assemble, finish slicing the leeks through at the root end. Arrange 2 halves in a circle around each fish fillet or chicken paillard. Garnish with a spoonful of your best hollandaise, mousseline, or light cream sauce.

AFTERTHOUGHT: I emphasize keeping an eye on the leeks as they cook—a minute too long and they will have lost their brilliant color and texture.

They are also delicious served chilled or at room temperature.

JEWEL WILPAN'S MARTINI ONIONS

This is the way Jewel does it. Watch out—these onions are addictive.

Pour the juice from a small jar of pickled onions (the kind you put in martinis, naturally) into a small saucepan, and bring to a boil over medium heat. While the juice is heating, place a teaspoon of rock sugar in the jar. When the pickling liquid is hot, pour it back over the onions. (Make sure the jar is at room temperature.) Put the lid on and let them stand for several days. Makes a great martini.

SCALLION OIL

About 1/4 cup

Scallion oil is held in very high regard by Chinese chefs to flavor fried fish. Try this pungent, fragrant oil to dress stir-fry dishes, vegetables, or Chinese chicken salad.

2 tablespoons peanut oil	*½ cup finely chopped scallions,*
2 tablespoons sesame oil	*including green tops*

Heat the oils together over high heat until very hot but not smoking. Add the scallions and turn off heat.

Cover and let the mixture rest for 20 minutes. Strain through a fine sieve or cheesecloth. Discard scallions.

Keep oil in a covered glass container in a cool place, or refrigerate.

4 Desserts: Wicked and Virtuous

CHOCOLATE TORTE SOUFFLÉ

Serves eight

THE chocolate cake.

½ *pound semisweet chocolate*
4 *tablespoons butter*
5 *eggs, separated*
2 *tablespoons flour*

¾ *cup sugar*
Pinch of salt
Powdered sugar for garnish

Preheat oven to 325°F. Butter and flour a genoise pan or 10-inch quiche pan and refrigerate.

Melt the chocolate and butter over hot water.

Combine yolks, flour, and sugar and beat thoroughly. Fold in the chocolate mixture.

Beat the whites until firm, add 1 tablespoon of the sugar and the pinch of salt and beat until they form peaks, but are not dry. Fold the whites into the chocolate mixture.

Pour the batter into the prepared pan and bake 1 hour and 15 minutes. Remove from the oven and cool on a rack. Don't worry, the center of the cake will sink and crack. Dust the cake with powdered sugar.

AFTERTHOUGHTS: Unsweetened whipped cream is a perfect accompaniment.

For a standing ovation, frost the cake with chocolate mousse and garnish with fresh raspberries.

GANACHE

1 1/2 cups

The ultimate chocolate sauce. Unabashedly luxurious, use it as a cake filling or frosting, sauce, fondue, or hot fudge extraordinaire. It will keep, refrigerated, for weeks. Because it hardens when chilled, bring it to room temperature or melt it over simmering water before using.

1 package (8 ounces) semisweet   *1 cup heavy cream or crème*
  chocolate, cut into small pieces   *fraîche*

Place chocolate pieces in a medium bowl. Bring cream to a boil and pour it over the chocolate. Let sit for 3 minutes.

Using a wire whisk, blend the mixture until smooth and shiny. Cool and use as needed.

AFTERTHOUGHTS: The better the chocolate, the better the ganache. Belgian chocolate is outrageously delicious.

Vary the flavor of ganache with Grand Marnier, Frangelico, Amaretto, or rum.

Serve chocolate fondue with angel food cake and a variety of fresh fruits: oranges, strawberries, pineapple. But remember, the first person who drops something into the fondue has to bring the champagne next time.

DESSERT ORANGES

Light, refreshing, and deliciously virtuous, they provide a lovely note on which to end a sumptuous meal.

6–8 oranges

Peel the oranges, removing all white pith. Slice into 1/4-inch rounds; remove seeds, if any. Arrange the slices attractively on a serving plate. Sprinkle with sugar to taste and any one of the following:

8 or 10 fresh mint leaves, chopped
1 tablespoon fresh rosemary leaves
Ground cinnamon to taste

¼ cup of your favorite liqueur such as Grand Marnier, Marsala, Maraschino, Cointreau. Or perhaps a drizzling of Armagnac or dark rum?

Now let them marinate about 2 hours, either in the refrigerator or at room temperature.

APPENDIX

Tips on Ingredients

BROTH OR STOCK

Good stock is one of the major secrets of good cooking. Sometimes, though, I don't have homemade on hand, but there are alternatives— namely Swanson's chicken and beef broths, both highly acceptable seconds. When a recipe calls for strong stock, it's a simple matter to improve them. For chicken stock: Pour canned broth into a large saucepan and add a whole, quartered onion, a peeled garlic clove, a celery rib with leaves, a few peppercorns, a pinch of thyme, and a couple of parsley sprigs. Bring to a boil, reduce heat, and simmer about 20 minutes. Boil down a bit, strain, and use as needed.

For beef stock: Same as above, but also add a small bay leaf, 2 cloves, and a chopped carrot.

Fish stock substitutes are clam broth (bottled and expensive), Japanese instant dashi powders (available in many grocery stores), and do try Knorr instant fish bouillon.

CHEESE

Always use the best cheese you can find and afford. Spurn the processed stuff, especially the grated, prefab Parmesan or Romano; grate your own.

CHILIES

Take care when handling hot chilies. Their volatile oils can burn skin and eyes. Wear rubber gloves if possible, or wash hands carefully after preparation. Pay particular attention not to touch your face with your hands during handling, whether gloved or not. Also, avoid inhaling pepper steam when sautéing or frying them. Stand back when adding liquid to cooking chilies!

CREAM

Unless otherwise noted, use heavy cream in these recipes. Avoid "ultra-pasteurized."

CRÈME FRAÎCHE

Crème fraîche is a cultured heavy cream with a delicate, slightly sour taste. Use it as a simple sauce for hot vegetables, add a dollop to salad dressings, over fruit desserts, and to add body and richness to sauces. The lactic acid in crème fraîche will also act to tenderize chicken without overpowering its flavor.

Crème fraîche is becoming increasingly available in grocery stores, but making it is really a snap. Combine 1 cup heavy cream and 2 tablespoons cultured buttermilk in a clean jar. Cover and store in a warm place overnight, or until thickened. Stir and refrigerate. It will keep a week or longer, though its tart flavor will continue to develop as it sits in the refrigerator.

FLOUR

Use all-purpose unless otherwise noted. And do try Wondra instant flour; it's terrific for thickening stews and some sauces—and no lumps, ever!

HERBS

Fresh wins hands-down every time. Some herbs, particularly basil, cilantro, and chives, do not dry well; and there is no excuse for ever using dried parsley. The other standard culinary ones seem to do fine—marjoram, thyme, rosemary, dill, and so on. Try Bert Greene's idea: chop the amount of dried herbs you need together with the same amount of parsley for a fresher taste.

Fresh herbs are increasingly available in markets, or, better yet, why not grow some of your own on a sunny windowsill, outside in pots, or in the garden?

Herbes de Provence, the queen of dried herbs, is available from most specialty food shops. Packed in small earthenware jars, it is a savory mixture of thyme, rosemary, savory, sage, lavender, and basil, and is used to flavor meats, fish, breads, whatever. If you can't find it, order it from H. Roth & Son, 1577 First Avenue, New York, New York 10028.

MUSSELS

Purchase only the mussels that are tightly closed. When you get them home, put them in a basin of cold water. Toss out any that have opened (they aren't fresh). About an hour before you are going to use them, scrub them well and pull off the beard from each one. Drop them back into fresh, cold water until you need them.

Remember that mussels need to be cooked only long enough for them to open, about 5 minutes. Discard any that remain closed after cooking. Strain or pour off broth carefully, leaving any sand behind.

If you can find the New Zealand mussels, by all means buy them—they are delicious and have beautiful green shells and deep orange flesh.

OLIVE OIL

Use extra virgin olive oil for seasoning and salads. Virgin olive oil is fine for sautéing. Sasso or Sagra are worthy brands.

ORIENTAL INGREDIENTS

As for soy sauce, Kikkoman is still a favorite. For the other, more exotic ingredients like Chinese sweetened black vinegar, red miso, Thai fish sauce, or five-spice powder, do search out an Oriental market or well-stocked supermarket. If you have neither in your area, order them by mail from:

THE BANGKOK MARKET, INC.
3718 E. 26th Street
Vernon, Ca. 90023
(213) 264-7990
(All Thai foods)

B & C MARKET
711 North Broadway
Los Angeles, Ca. 90012
(213) 680-9760
(Chinese and most Oriental foods)

PIE CRUST

I have provided a recipe for short crust pastry on page 90. On the other hand, I tend to use Betty Crocker pie crust mix these days.

TOMATOES

Choose red, ripe, fresh tomatoes whenever possible. If unavailable, the next best thing would be canned Italian plum tomatoes; Progresso is excellent. And try Pomi tomato purée; very fresh tasting.

When using ripe tomatoes, don't bother peeling them unless they are to be used in long-cooked dishes or for coulis.

And be on the lookout for pumate, heavenly sun-dried tomatoes packed in olive oil. Try some in sauces, salads, pasta dishes, sandwiches; their explosive tomato flavor is glorious.

Horticulture
GARLIC

> A bulbous herb *(Allium sativum)* of the lily family widely cultivated for its pungent compound bulbs much used in cookery.
> —Webster's Dictionary

Garlic is fairly simple to grow, given reasonable attention; though why in the world anyone would want to escapes me given the availability of the bulb. Two or more million tons of it are grown yearly and delivered fresh and spicy to every market, large and small. But in case you feel inclined to grow your own just for the hell of it, here's how:

What: Obtain mother bulbs or "sets" from mail-order seed houses or nurseries, or simply obtain fresh bulbs from your local grocer. Separate the bulbs into cloves, making sure they are firm and fresh.

When: Northern gardeners should plant sets in the fall so the root system can develop before the ground freezes; it will sprout come spring. (Mulch during the coldest part of winter.) The rest of the country can plant in early spring.

Where: In full sun, in well-drained, loose, somewhat rich soil.

How: Plant cloves 1 inch deep and at least 3 inches apart, in rows 12 inches apart. Or plant here and there in the garden, especially around such ornamentals as rose bushes, as the resulting plants help keep aphids and other pests at bay. Harvest as usual, but carefully.

Keep well watered the first three weeks. When shoots are up and going strong continue watering every 3 to 5 days, and continue until you see the stalks beginning to emerge. Then begin to cut back water or bulbs will rot.

Harvesting: Bulbs can take nine months to a year to reach maturity, so don't give up hope. When the leaves begin to brown, stop watering. Don't worry, the cloves will continue growing. When the tops die down, gently dig them up with a pitchfork (or hand tool, for that matter). Let them cure on the ground for a day or two, making sure you dig them up during a dry period. After they've cured, braid the dried stalks, hang them up on your kitchen wall, and gloat.

Insect Repellent: Garlic has almost no pests of its own. It is also the base of an excellent insect repellent for everything from house plants to vegetables. Simply whirl 10 or 12 cloves with a cup of water in the blender. Strain through cheesecloth and add a few drops of liquid soap. (Toss the gleanings around the base of outdoor plants). Store in a glass container, covered, in the refrigerator. When you wish to use it, dilute with water 10 to 1 to start. Experiment to find the right strength for your particular pest. Spray on affected plants, being careful to spray undersides of leaves as well. Reapply as needed.

You can also vary this discourager by adding onion, hot peppers, and chilies to the original recipe.

ONIONS

A widely cultivated Asiatic herb *(Allium cepa)*
of the lily family with pungent edible bulbs.
—Webster's Dictionary

Considering the availability and variety of sweet, fresh onions and their inordinately long growing season (a biennial, they take almost two years from seed to harvest, or from onion sets one full season), I suggest you buy them and forget farming. If you insist on growing your own, there are plenty of fine volumes on vegetable gardening.

LEEKS

> A biennial garden herb *(Allium porrum)* of the
> lily family grown for its mildly pungent succu-
> lent linear leaves and esp. for its thick cylindri-
> cal stalk.
>   —Webster's Dictionary

In Europe, this "poor man's asparagus" is a staple. You'll find they're easy
to grow.

When: Sow seeds as soon as ground can be worked.

Where: In full sun in well-drained, loose, fertile soil.

How: Plant seeds 1/4 inch deep and about 2 inches apart in rows 18
inches apart. As seedlings appear, thin them gradually to 6 inches apart.
Toss seedlings in your salads or use them like scallions. Keep the little
darlings moist and weeded.

Harvesting: Leeks can be enjoyed at any stage of growth; dig them up
as you need them. Where winters are severe, mulch them, and dig them
up throughout the winter. Note that they take 70 to 130 days, depending
on variety.

Blanching: This is the continual hilling up of soil around the plant to
produce longer whites (and dirtier leeks). Since you are probably using
them as fast as you can, you won't want to bother with blanching. But if
you do, get a book on gardening if you're interested in this process.

SHALLOTS

> A bulbous perennial herb *(Allium ascalonicum)*
> that resembles an onion and produces small
> clustered bulbs used in seasoning.
>   —Webster's Dictionary

Sweet and delicate in flavor with tender lavender bulbs, the shallot is fussy
to grow and tenuous to store. If your gardening fantasies include growing
these, investigate a good book on vegetable gardening. Otherwise, give
the space over to scallions and chives.

SCALLIONS

A young onion pulled before the bulb has en-
larged and used esp. in salads.
                    —Webster's Dictionary

Now here is a worthy for your green thumb. Remarkably easy to grow with a rapid and almost 100 percent harvest. Also called bunching onions, green onions, or, more appropriately, spring onions, as their slender, tender shoots begin appearing in early spring. Purists argue that a scallion is an adolescent green onion. I say they're all the same—delicious.

When: In early spring as soon as the ground is workable.

Where: In full sun, in well-drained, loose, somewhat rich soil.

How: Plant seeds directly in the garden (or a planter box or tub). Sow them thinly; they all seem to germinate. Thin to 2 to 3 inches apart. Keep well watered and weeded until they're ready to harvest.

Harvesting: When the tops are 6 or 8 inches long, lift them right out of the soil. Drop a seed where the vacancy exists to keep a supply going.

CHIVES

A perennial plant *(Allium schoenoprasum)*
related to the onion.
                    —Webster's Dictionary

A shoo-in to grow—no bulb to worry about, as only the stalks are used for cooking, unlike the rest of the family.

When: Anytime in pots, early spring in the garden.

Where: Full sun, good soil.

What: Seeds or clumps of chives from gardening centers.

How: Sow seeds in a 6-inch or larger pot, filled with good potting soil. Sprinkle 20 or so seeds around and cover lightly with soil. Water gently, especially at first so you do not disturb seeds. Plant similarly in the garden. Or transplant clumps to pot or ground.

Harvest: Snip them off 2 inches from the bottom with scissors. Every two years, divide the clump and transplant to fresh soil.

INDEX